TAMANAWIS SECONDARY
12600 - 66 Avenue
Surrey, B.C. V3W 2A8

The World of Mark...

A Canadian Perspective

Student Workbook

The World of Marketing
A Canadian Perspective

Student Workbook

Authors

David Notman

Jack Wilson

Writers

David DeSantis

Greg Gregoriou

John Pownall

Adele Schiedel

THOMSON

★

NELSON

Australia   Canada   Mexico   Singapore   Spain   United Kingdom   United States

THOMSON

NELSON

The World of Marketing: A Canadian Perspective
Student Workbook

David Notman and Jack Wilson

Director of Publishing
David Steele

Publisher
Mark Cressman

Executive Managing Editor, Production
Nicola Balfour

Program Manager
Norma Kennedy

Developmental Editor
Su Mei Ku

Editorial Assistant
Kim Kirby

Production Editor
Debbie Wright

Production Coordinator
Helen Locsin

Cover Design
Johanna Liburd

Composition
Kyle Gell Design

Permissions
Paula Joiner

Printer
Webcom

Copyright © 2003 by Nelson, a division of Thomson Canada Limited.

Printed and bound in Canada
1   2   3   4   05   04   03   02

For more information contact Nelson, 1120 Birchmount Road, Toronto, Ontario, M1K 5G4.
Or you can visit our Internet site at http://www.nelson.com

All rights reserved. No part of this work covered by the copyright herein may be reproduced, transcribed, or used in any form or by any means—graphic, electronic, or mechanical, including photocopying, recording, taping, Web distribution, or information storage and retrieval systems—without the written permission of the publisher.

For permission to use material from this text or product, contact us by
Tel 1-800-730-2214
Fax 1-800-730-2215
www.thomsonrights.com

Every effort has been made to trace ownership of all copyrighted material and to secure permission from copyright holders. In the event of any question arising as to the use of any material, we will be pleased to make the necessary corrections in future printings.

National Library of Canada Cataloguing in Publication Data

Notman, David
   The world of marketing: a Canadian perspective. Student workbook / David Notman and Jack Wilson.

ISBN 0-17-625948-1

1. Marketing—Problems, exercises, etc.
2. Marketing—Canada—Problems, exercises, etc. I. Wilson, Jack II. Title.

HF5415.12.C3N68 2002 Suppl. 2   658.8
C2002-903874-X

TABLE OF CONTENTS

Chapter 7   Pricing   126

Chapter 8   Distribution and Logistics   146

Chapter 9
Advertising, Promotion, and Sales   167

CHAPTER 1: What Is Marketing?

A. Understanding Key Terms: Chapter Introduction

Before reading this chapter, write what you think each term means in the middle column of this chart. After reading this chapter, complete the column on the right. How do your definitions and the textbook's compare?

Term	What Do You Think It Means?	Definition from Text
marketing		
consumer market		
raw materials		
processed goods		
target market		
marketing concept		
tariffs		
distribution management		
marketing mix		
value equation		
push strategy		
pull strategy		

Read Section 1.1, **Marketing Goods and Services** (pages 3–8), in your textbook, then fill in the missing information in this chart.

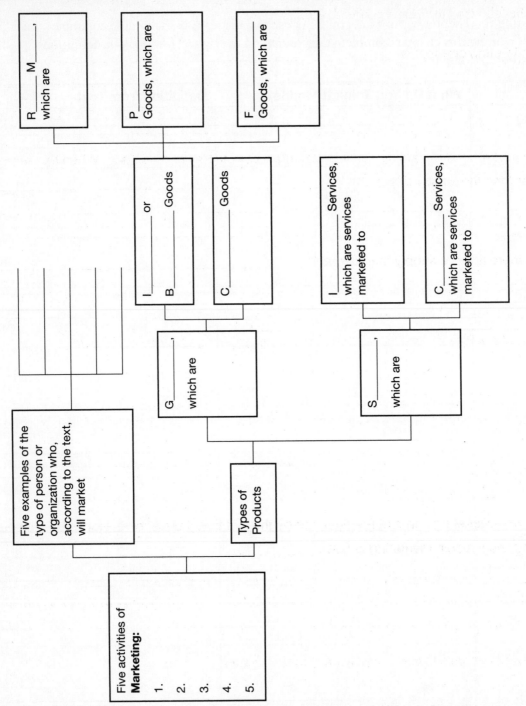

The difference between industrial and consumer goods and services is

_____

A target market is

_____

C. Understanding the Ideas:
1.2 Evolution of the Marketing Concept

Read Section 1.2, **Evolution of the Marketing Concept** (pages 8–10), in your textbook and complete the following information as you read.

1. The marketing concept is _____
_____
_____
_____

2. The importance of marketing activities changes with supply and demand. When the demand is greater than the supply of goods, _____
_____
_____

3. When there is more supply than demand, _____
_____
_____

4. The Industrial Revolution changed the balance of supply and demand because_____
_____
_____

5. As a result, marketing changed during the late 1800s and 1900s. Marketing started to concentrate on
_____
_____
_____

6. Today, the marketing concept is influenced by the fact that production in North America outstrips demand. As a result, marketing is now _____
_____
_____
_____

Record two new concepts that you have learned in this section.

1. _____
_____

2. _____
_____

Read the following comic strip and comment on the two statements below.

1. A successful business or brand is not dependent on a revolutionary new concept.

_____
_____
_____
_____
_____
_____
_____
_____
_____
_____

2. The world of marketing surrounds us.

_____
_____
_____
_____
_____
_____
_____
_____
_____

E. Understanding the Ideas: 1.3 Marketing and the Organization

Read Section 1.3, **Marketing and the Organization** (pages 12–14), in your textbook, then complete the following chart.

	Marketing and the Organization
regional organization	Definition: Example:
international organization	Definition: Example:
brand management	Definition: Example:
distribution management	Definition: Example:

What is one thing you have learned in this section?

_____

_____

_____

_____

F. Understanding the Ideas: 1.4 Marketing Activities

Complete the following outline as you read Section 1.4, **Marketing Activities** (pages 16–17), in your textbook.

Marketing Activities

A. _____

    1. Conducting surveys gathers

       a) Preferences

       b) _____

       c) _____

       d) _____

B. _____

    1. Three concerns of the P _____

       D_____ team

       a) _____

       b) _____

       c) _____

C. P _____

D. P _____

E. Branding

    1. Branding includes a product's

       a) _____

       b) _____

       c) _____

       d) _____

       e) _____

F. S _____

G. P_____ D_____

    1. A company must be able to ship its product

       a) _____

       b) _____

H. I_____ M_____

    1. A company tries to have

       a) enough inventory to cover sales

       b) _____

I. Storage

    1. _____

J. _____

    1. Advertising

    2. _____

As you read Section 1.5, **Consumer and Competitive Markets** (pages 19–20), in your textbook, complete the following information about the different types of markets.

A consumer market is _____
_____
_____
_____
_____
_____
_____
_____
_____
_____
_____
_____
_____

A competitive market is _____
_____
_____
_____
_____
_____
_____
_____
_____
_____
_____
_____
_____

An aggregate market is _____
_____
_____
_____
_____
_____
_____
_____
_____
_____
_____
_____
_____

A differentiated market is _____
_____
_____
_____
_____
_____
_____
_____
_____
_____
_____
_____
_____

H. Charting Examples: Target Marketing

Complete the following chart by 1) providing a *specific* example of the organization or person given in the left-hand column, and 2) suggesting the market your example would target. The first one has been done for you.

Organization or Individual	Example	Target Market
clothing retailer	Le Chateau	Young, fashion conscious people, aged 14–25. This store targets "early adopters" who have a fashion-forward, leading-edge image.
shoe retailer		
fast-food restaurant		
recording artist		
non-profit organization		
politician		
industry of your choice: _____ _____ _____		
industry of your choice: _____ _____ _____		

Record information about each of the 4 Ps as you read Section 1.6, **The Marketing Mix** (pages 21–24), in your textbook.

The Marketing Mix—The 4 Ps

P_____ includes
_____
_____
_____
_____
_____
_____
_____
_____
_____
_____
_____
_____

P_____ includes
_____
_____
_____
_____
_____
_____
_____
_____
_____
_____
_____
_____

P_____ includes
_____
_____
_____
_____
_____
_____
_____
_____
_____
_____
_____

P_____ includes
_____
_____
_____
_____
_____
_____
_____
_____
_____
_____
_____

J. Ranking the 4 Ps: The Marketing Mix

Every company will consider all 4 Ps of marketing, but they will put emphasis on different ones, depending on the product and situation. For each of the organizations in the chart below, rank the importance of each of the 4 Ps (1 being the most important and 4 being the least important). Explain your ranking.

Then research two of the organizations (using print and electronic sources) and write a short report on whether your findings support your rankings.

	Product/ Service	Promotion	Price	Place	Explanation
Air Canada					
Jacob					
Danier					
The Gap					
Aldo Shoes					
Nike					
Pepsi					
Hostess					
Tim Hortons					
Green Peace					

The following is the beginning of a mind map for Section 1.7, **Marketing Strategies** (pages 24–30), in your textbook. As you read this section, complete the mind map. Add lines as necessary.

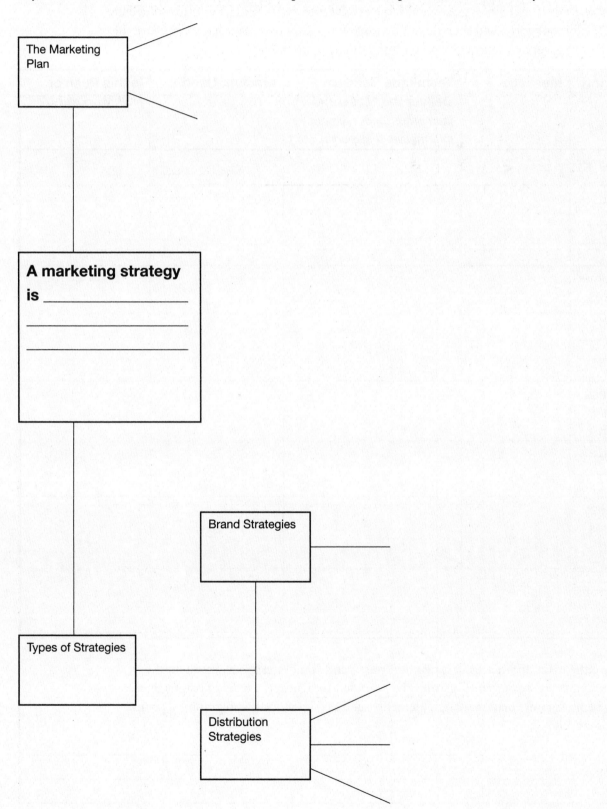

L. Comparing Advertisements: Distribution Strategies

1. Review several advertisements for each of the categories in the left-hand column of the chart below. (You may have to look at a trade magazine, such as *Marketing, Canadian Business,* or *Profit,* for business goods and services advertisements.) Select one advertisement for each of the categories and then fill in the remaining columns in the chart. Compare the advertising messages and strategies used for the different markets.

Category	Message	Technique Used to Deliver the Message *(humorous, endorsement, informative, testimonial, etc.)*	Medium Used	Is this Push or Pull Marketing?
consumer goods Ad for: _____ _____				
consumer services Ad for: _____ _____				
business goods Ad for: _____ _____				
business services Ad for: _____ _____				

2. What are the main differences between the "push" and "pull" strategies, based on the advertisements you reviewed? Consider the intended audience, the level of language, the level of technical information, design elements such as colour, font, and graphics, promotional offers, etc.

_____

_____

_____

_____

Read the article and answer the questions that follow.

From Recalled to Requested

How B.C.'s Fleetwood Sausage used marketing to rebound from a crisis over tainted meat products

By Stephen Abbott

In the 1990s, Fleetwood Sausage was a typical bulk meat producer, pounding out generic products to major grocery chains. Creating products based on traditional European recipes, the little family-run operation in Surrey, B.C., had become too big, and was ultimately acquired by the eastern industry giant, J.M. Schneider. Low prices and volume sales were the key ingredients in this game of margins. Profitability for product lines was more about production management and cost control than marketing. It was a stable situation, but there was little room for error, let alone risk.

All of a sudden, in 1999 there was error. Perhaps even a crisis. Tainted products were suddenly and loudly recalled, and sales plummeted. The little company that had never made headlines was the lead story on the news—and nobody liked what was being said.

Clearly, Fleetwood wouldn't be the first company to go through a crisis like this. Others have survived worse predicaments and carried on (sometimes limping along) just as they did before. Just advertise that the problem was corrected, and all it would take was a little time, right?

Wrong. Fleetwood's dramatic turnaround isn't about doing things as others have done. This story is about the most important ingredient in the development of a new brand: a believer. Fleetwood's unlikely believer is Mike.

Mike McRae had worked for Fleetwood Sausage for 17 years, starting as a pepperoni cutter and working his way up to marketing manager. When Mike approached Vancouver's WOW! a Branding Company, he had nothing to lose and one very clear goal: to make Fleetwood Sausage into something special. Mike's strategy for recovery was simple and aggressive: reduce product SKUs, regain control of product selection, and reposition the products with exciting new identities.

Mike finally had the ability to do it his way. For the first time, Fleetwood's marketing strategy was treated to proper tools such as consumer research and creative briefs. Keeping creative control on the West Coast was critical (as opposed to getting lost in the shuffle back east). It was

important to Mike that the creative was distinct and radical—a "do it first and beg for forgiveness later" approach. And he wanted to be face-to-face with the creative team.

Fleetwood had decided to take the high road on quality, but it was WOW! that challenged Mike to focus the brand on the experience, not just the flavour. He agreed, and the product lineup took on a radical new approach.

Prepared meats are used for a variety of occasions, and WOW!'s goal was to draw on the customer's experience. It started with one line—hearty whole meat products that we affectionately named Prospector, a reference to the boldness of the manly gold rush era. Next in line was Asian Express, the families of Authentic and Private Reserve salamis and, of course, sausages.

Limited budgets are always a factor, and consumer advertising was out of the question. With each product line, dynamic new packaging was created to help tell the story of the experience and allow the product to visually jump off the shelf. We purposely downplayed the Fleetwood name and brought individual life to each product identity. In response, major grocery chains started to create special sections for "branded" meats.

Eye-catching trade sheets and exciting POP materials brought the new life of the brand into the stores. Fleetwood Phil, a sausage mascot for the new direction, was created for both internal and external promotional activities.

Retailers and the head office in Toronto are taking note—and for good reason. In a world that measures success in obscure phrases like "contribution weights," product lines are seeing increases of up to 100%. Consumers have shown a willingness to pay the higher price for the experience, and that translates into more for everybody.

But the Fleetwood brand's success doesn't stop there. Mike has allowed the renegade approach to infiltrate every aspect of Fleetwood's business. Everything from annual presentations to promotional videos is treated to Mike's unstoppable enthusiasm. No one knows what to expect. At WOW!, we know that the success of a brand starts with a good idea, and a believer. At Fleetwood, Mike is the ultimate brand hero.

By fighting conventional wisdom at every level, Mike has generated a buzz across the company best summed up by a simple statement from his boss, sales manager Jeff Parker, "Mike, you make me nervous." Interestingly, Mike hasn't had to beg for forgiveness yet.

Source: Marketing Magazine, *March 11, 2002*

1. What was the *main problem* facing Fleetwood Sausage in 1999?

   _____

   _____

2. Complete the chart below for Fleetwood Sausage.

The Marketing Mix—the 4Ps	Pre-Crisis Strategy *(You may have to make some assumptions not included in the case.)*	Recommended Post-Crisis Strategy	Anticipated Effectiveness
P RICE	The price of the products. Check the competition. Price accordingly.	Change prices if item does not sell. supply / demand	
P RODUCT			
P ROMOTION			
P LACE			

3. Classify the following marketing activities used by Fleetwood as being a push, pull, or combination strategy. Explain your answer in the right-hand column.

Activity	Classification—Push, Pull, or Combination	Explanation
new packaging		
point of purchase (POP) materials		
trade sheets (data for stores and wholesalers)		

Crossword

Use the clues below to solve the following crossword.

Across

1. A category of goods that is also called business goods

6. A distribution strategy that attempts to increase consumer demand directly

8. This outlines how a company will carry out its marketing plan

10. A common method of organizing marketing activities used by companies that sell many brands (2 words)

12. Type of media including magazines and radio that became available to advertisers in the early/mid 1900s (2 words)

13. This Canadian company processes over 450 tonnes of potatoes every hour

14. This part of the marketing mix includes inventory management and channel selection

15. An organization marketing their cause to potential donors and their benefits to potential clients

16. A marketing strategy focussed on selling the product to retailers, importers, or wholesalers

Down

2. Markets that are characterized in a specific way (e.g., income, personal values, gender, or age) (2 words)

3. A group of consumers to whom marketers want to sell their products (2 words)

4. The official term for import taxes

5. Canadian firms that sell abroad and/or buy from other nations are participating in this market (2 words)

7. This allows businesses and consumers to complete transactions without ever seeing one another

8. A type of promotional tool that marketers use in a supermarket environment

9. This adds together all the benefits and subtracts the costs involved in obtaining a product (2 words)

10. In addition to research and packaging, one of the most important elements of the product mix

11. This refers to the four Ps of marketing (2 words)

True/False

Circle T if the statement is true, F if it is false.

1. As a result of the uniqueness of the product, Jones Soda is not considered to be in a competitive market.   T   F

2. Some companies have separate marketing plans for consumer and industrial goods, even if they are the same brand/product.   T   F

3. Integrated circuit boards are a raw material as well as a finished good.   T   F

4. In 2000, Canadian exports sustained approximately one in three Canadian jobs and represented 45% of everything produced in Canada.   T   F

5. When supply is high, excessive marketing is redundant because the product sells itself.   T   F

Fill in the Blanks

1. Marketing is the sum of all the activities involved in the _____, _____, _____, _____, and _____ of goods and services to satisfy consumer needs and wants.

2. Non-profit organizations market their cause to potential _____ and their benefits to potential _____.

3. Companies may organize their marketing divisions by region, _____, _____, method of _____, or a combination of these.

O. Marketing Plan: Getting Started

Read page 34 in your textbook, **Marketing Plan**. Then complete these activities to help you get started with your own marketing plan.

1. List five possible products, services, ideas, or nonprofit causes that you are considering for your marketing plan. Once you have listed your ideas, gather feedback on them from at least five different people. In the last column of the chart, rate the ideas based on the feedback you received.

Concept	Comments from at least five people	Rating

2. From the initial five ideas, select the idea that you rated highest. Create a more detailed picture of your product, service, or cause by filling in the following chart.

Industry *(Type of Product, Service, or Cause)*	Description of the Product, Service, or Cause	Description of the Target Market

3. Consider possible goals for your product, service, or cause and record them in the chart below. Note that you may have both primary and secondary goals. Identify strategies designed to achieve each of these goals. This should be done for each of your goals even though you may decide not to implement all of them. While doing this exercise, be sure to keep the marketing mix, the market, and the competition in mind.

Goals	Strategies
Primary Goals	Strategy 1:
	Strategy 2:
	Strategy 3:
Secondary Goals	Strategy 1:
	Strategy 2:
	Strategy 3:

4. List some techniques that you would consider using to try to create interest and enthusiasm about your product in the marketplace. For example, you might consider mascots, special promotional offers, tie-ins with other companies, unique sampling programs, etc.

_____

_____

_____

_____

_____

_____

_____

5. Do a **SWOT** analysis on your idea. That is, describe your product, service, or cause's greatest **S**trength, **W**eakness, **O**pportunity, and **T**hreat.

a) Greatest Strength: _____

_____

_____

b) Greatest Weakness: _____

_____

_____

c) Greatest Opportunity:_____

_____

_____

d) Greatest Threat: _____

_____

_____

CHAPTER 2: The Consumer

A. Understanding Key Terms: Chapter Introduction

Before reading this chapter, write what you think each term means in the middle column of this chart. After reading this chapter, complete the column on the right. How do your definitions and the textbook's compare?

Term	What Do You Think It Means?	Definition from Text
consumer		
product life cycle		
shelf allowance		
fad		
niche market		
trend		
consumer segment		
demographics		
nesters		
baby boomers		
family life cycle		
buying process		
industrial consumer		

B. Understanding the Ideas: 2.1 Consumer Demand

Read Section 2.1, **Consumer Demand** (pages 37–40), in your textbook and use the following to help guide your notetaking.

A *consumer* is _____

A *customer* is _____

A consumer is not necessarily a customer. Explain the concept of a *gatekeeper*. _____

_____

_____

_____

Every person has both *wants* and *needs*. The difference between these two is _____

_____

_____

_____

_____

_____

Explain what is meant by "wants and needs can vary depending on the person, the place, and the timing." Provide two examples where the demand for a product might change because of changing circumstances.

_____

_____

_____

_____

_____

_____

_____

_____

_____

_____

_____

_____

_____

_____

_____

As you read Section 2.2, **Product Life Cycles** (pages 41–49), in your textbook, build on the following map to provide yourself with a study and recall tool. The map has been started for you, but you will have to add lines and concepts.

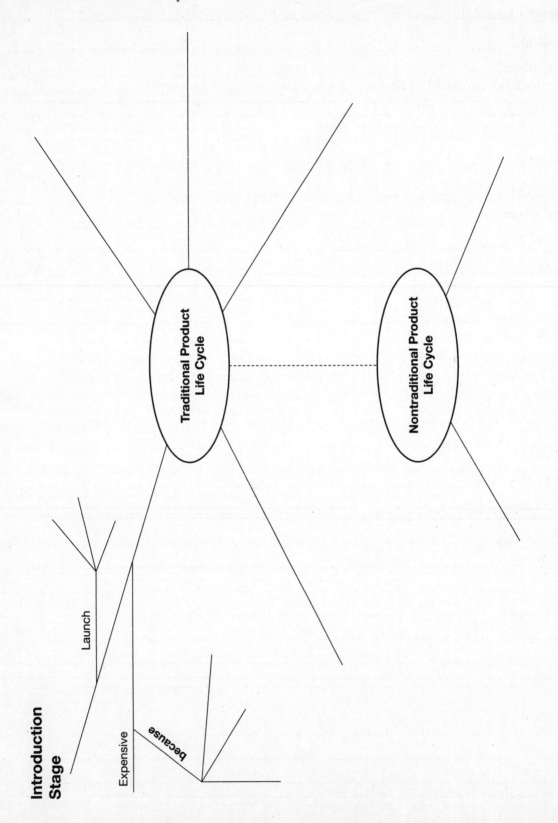

D. Making Connections: The Product Life Cycle and the 4 Ps

The marketing mix for a product changes at each stage of its life cycle. In the space provided, explain how each of the marketing mix elements is affected and why.

1. **Introduction** (e.g., Promotion: heavy promotion to ensure product awareness)

   Product:_____

   Promotion: _____

   Price: _____

   Place:_____

2. **Growth**

   Product:_____

   Promotion: _____

   Price: _____

   Place:_____

3. **Maturity**

   Product:_____

   Promotion: _____

   Price: _____

   Place:_____

4. **Decline**

   Product:_____

   Promotion: _____

   Price: _____

   Place:_____

E. Understanding the Ideas: 2.3 The Consumer Market

As you read Section 2.3, **The Consumer Market** (pages 50–65), in your textbook, fill in the missing information and complete the chart below.

A consumer profile is _____

_____

Consumers sharing common characteristics represent a _____

_____

Marketers use this information to identify two types of markets. Name and describe them. _____

_____

_____

The Consumer Market			
Demographics	**Psychographics**	**Geographics**	**Product Use Statistics**

How has this section changed your view of how products are marketed? _____

_____

_____

F. Charting Products: Demographics

1. Fill in the following chart for each of the products in the first column.

Product or Service	Age Group[1]	Gender M, F, B (Both)	Family Life Cycle[2]	Income Level	Ethnicity and Cultural Considerations? (e.g., Are there numbers that you might want to avoid on houses? Colours? Design?)	Comments and Observations
skateboard						
house						
make-up						
life insurance						
cruise						
set of fine china						
Registered Education Savings Plan (RESP)						
portable music player						
crib						

[1] The age groups outlined by Statistics Canada are <15, 15–24, 25–44, 45–64, 65–74, and 75 and over. The product may be of interest to people in more than one of the categories. Indicate which age group you feel is the primary market and then note any secondary markets in the Comments and Observations column. If you feel the product is of equal interest to all age groups, enter "A" in the Age Group column.

[2] The product may be of interest to people in more than one of the Family Life Cycle categories. In this case, enter the top two stages in which you feel the product would be of most interest, and provide your reasoning in the Comments and Observations column.

Read the article and answer the questions that follow.

Forget the hip, focus on the oldsters with money

Latest generation of marketers falls into an old trap

By Mark Solomons and Annie Counsell

There seems to be a widely held belief that success in the online world will come from grabbing as many young, hip, and trendy customers as possible, says Stephen Dull, a partner in Accenture's (formerly Andersen Consulting) eBranding practice.

"In fact, 10% of the US population accounts for 70% of all online spending, and the heavyweight spenders are between 35 and 44 years of age. The new marketing strategy should be to forget the eyeballs and focus on the wallets. We were all seduced."

It appears the latest generation of e-marketers has fallen into a trap that their old-economy counterparts have been aware of for years: trying to address a hip, youthful audience when they should be thinking about another group of people altogether. No wonder their messages have turned out to be largely inappropriate.

The problem, Mr. Dull says, is all too familiar. Marketers have fallen into the trap of trying too hard to sell to people like themselves. "Too many e-marketers were looking in the mirror instead of at their target audience," he says.

Underneath that, however, Accenture's research suggests that the e-marketing effort has failed to project an inclusive message that may have appeal to a broader, older, and crucially more affluent audience.

There are incontrovertible demographic trends behind the results of Mr. Dull's survey of more than 2000 online consumers, which was conducted by Accenture's eBranding practice in cooperation with Online Insight of the US.

These trends are ones that even the most creative minds will not be able to influence: The population as a whole is getting older. Rising life expectancy, lower birth rates, and the effects of the postwar Baby Boom will converge during the next 20 years to produce a bulge in the number of people over 50.

Many people in these expanding age groups are richer than ever. The long economic upswing of the later 1990s has disproportionately benefited those with savings, personal investments, and inherited, mostly property-based wealth.

Compared with their own parents at the same age, the over-50s are healthier, better-educated, and much more affluent. A great number of them have far more money than younger consumers, and they are more active than any previous generation. So what if they do not get out to night clubs quite as much?

The challenge is to develop products and ways of selling them that will acknowledge age without overtly drawing attention to it and will resist the temptation to set out its pitch in direct opposition to the values of the young.

"The wish to portray self and maintain sexuality among older people has increased very much in the last 20 years," says Peter Cooper, a psychologist and chief executive of CRAM International, a London-based market research company. He notes that sales of toiletries, cosmetics, and clothing have increased markedly among people over age 50.

While there are positive images of older age groups in advertising, they remain rare. More common are complaints that portrayals of the elderly, particularly in campaigns aimed at the young, are routinely offensive and inappropriate.

It is increasingly being recognized that simply aiming a marketing or advertising campaign at "the elderly" is far too simplistic and that there is a large number of subgroups with that category.

"To some extent this is about 'cohorts', not age," says Sally Ford-Hutchinson, an advertising consultant.

"There will be a variety of attitudes dependent on psychological make-up and upbringing. Some people in their 40s behave as if they're 20, and everyone thinks they are 10 years younger than they really are."

Source: Financial Times

1. a) What does Stephen Dull say is the widely held belief about success in the online world?

   _____

   _____

   b) Using information from the article, as well as your own knowledge and experience, either defend or dispute Dull's argument.

   _____

   _____

   _____

   _____

   c) What age group accounts for most online spending? Why?

   _____

   _____

   _____

   _____

2. Consider the following statement: "It is increasingly being recognized that simply aiming a marketing or advertising campaign at 'the elderly' is far too simplistic and that there is a large number of sub-groups within that category." In the chart below, suggest *four* "sub-groups" of the elderly category for which you could develop an e-marketing campaign. Give each sub-group a name and describe it with respect to its demographic and psychographic characteristics. For example: **F.A.A.T.'ies**—Fit and Active Types; **M&M's**—Medically Dependent and Merry; **W.O.O.P'ies**—Well Off Older People. Then suggest a couple of products that you may try marketing to them.

Sub-group 1: _____	Sub-group 2: _____
Demographics:	Demographics:
Psychographics:	Psychographics:
Products:	Products:
Sub-group 3: _____	Sub-group 4: _____
Demographics:	Demographics:
Psychographics:	Psychographics:
Products:	Products:

H. Writing a Memo: Geographics

As the vice president of marketing, you and your company plan to market the *same* product or service (your choice) to urban, suburban, and rural customers. Write a short memo to the president of your company outlining how you are going to overcome the geographic obstacles. Use the space below to plan your memo.

_____

_____

_____

_____

_____

_____

_____

I. Charting Product Users: Product Use Statistics

Imagine that you are a marketer for video games. For each of the age groups in the chart below, indicate whether you would consider this group to be light to medium, heavy, or non-users of your product. Use Y for yes, N for no, and P for possible. Explain your answer in the last column. If you choose "No Plans to Use" for any of the groups, try to think of a way that you could position your product to make it of more interest.

Age	Light to Medium	Heavy	Non-User		Rationale
			First-Time Users	No Plans to Use	
< 15					
15–24					
25–44					
45–64					
65–74					
75 and over					

J. Understanding the Ideas: 2.4 Consumer Motivation

As you read Section 2.4, **Consumer Motivation** (pages 67–70), in your textbook, describe the following:

Thorndike's Law of Effect: _____

_____

_____

_____

_____

_____

_____

_____

Maslow's Hierarchy of Needs: _____

1. _____

2. _____

3. _____

4. _____

5. _____

Alderfer's ERG Theory: _____

_____

_____

_____

_____

_____

_____

What have you learned in this section? _____

_____

_____

_____

_____

_____

_____

_____

K. Applying Knowledge:
Thorndike's Law of Effect and Maslow's Hierarchy of Needs

1. What might a marketer do to help reduce the negative feelings suggested by Thorndike's Law of Effect when a consumer purchases the following?

   an expensive luxury car _____

   _____

   a laptop computer _____

   _____

   a mutual fund that has lost 10% of its value in two weeks _____

   _____

2. Develop five different slogans for a single product that will each appeal to a different level in Maslow's Hierarchy of Needs (e.g., for a sports drink, the slogan "The ultimate thirst quencher" appeals to physiological needs; the slogan "Have no fear, the thirst eliminator is here!" appeals to safety needs). Indicate which of Maslow's levels the slogan appeals to.

   _____

   _____

   _____

   _____

   _____

   _____

   _____

   _____

   _____

   _____

3. Select five print advertisements from newspapers or magazines. In the chart below, identify which level of Maslow's Hierarchy of Needs the advertisement appeals to and discuss how this is achieved. Is the advertisement effective? Why or why not?

Level of Maslow's Hierarchy	Explanation

Read Section 2.5, **The Buying Decision** (pages 71–72), in your textbook. Fill in the Buying Decision diagram below and discuss the significance of each step in relation to major purchases, shopping goods, and impulse items. What did you learn?

M. Making Connections: The Buying Process

A young couple has just had triplets and is looking to purchase a minivan. They are considering models in the $25 000 to $35 000 range. Help the couple through each step of the buying-decision process.

Step 1. What is the situation? _____

_____

_____

Step 2. Outline four specific criteria that will be most important when making the purchase decision (e.g., size, cup holders, etc.).

i) _____

ii) _____

iii) _____

iv) _____

Step 3. Research three minivans from different automakers. Organize your data into a chart like the one below.

	Minivan #1	Minivan #2	Minivan #3
Criteria (i)			
Criteria (ii)			
Criteria (iii)			
Criteria (iv)			

Step 4. The Decision: Which of the minivans should they purchase? _____

Step 5. The Purchase: The couple has only $15 000 in savings. How would they finance the rest of the purchase? What could/do marketers of minivans do to overcome this obstacle?

_____

_____

_____

_____

Step 6. Evaluation: Fill in the following chart. On what basis would the couple evaluate its purchase? How could this purchase become either a positive or negative experience as outlined by Thorndike's Law of Effect? In the last column, discuss what strategy a marketer could use to make sure that the purchasers' experience is positive.

Basis for Evaluation	Positive Experience	Negative Experience	Marketing Strategy

Creating an Advertisement: Motivational Theories

Imagine that you are now trying to market this same minivan to the couple in the last activity. Create a print advertisement for the minivan. Do the following exercises as you create your advertisement.

1. Describe your target market. _____
   _____

2. Appealing to your market:

   a) How will your advertisement use:

      rational forces? _____
      _____
      _____

      emotional forces?_____
      _____
      _____

      social forces? _____
      _____
      _____

   b) What step in the buying decision will you emphasize? Why? _____
      _____
      _____
      _____
      _____

c) Provide three different possible approaches to your advertisement, each of which will appeal to one of the three levels of needs in Alderfer's ERG Theory.

Existence Needs: _____

_____

Relatedness Needs: _____

_____

Growth Needs: _____

_____

d) Decide on one of the approaches that you outlined in part c), and create a thumbnail sketch of your advertisement. Include the copy for your advertisement in the space provided.

3. Find a promotional piece that has actually been produced by the automaker for the minivan you chose. You may find this in print or on the Internet. What are the similarities and differences between your advertisement and the one you found? Is one advertisement necessarily better than the other, or do the differences just reflect a different marketing strategy?

Similarities	Differences	Explanation

4. Consider the changes you would have to make if you were marketing this minivan to the industrial/institutional consumer. How would your approach to the advertisement change if you were marketing your minivan to a company that wanted to lease the minivan for making deliveries?

_____

_____

_____

_____

_____

N. Understanding the Ideas:
2.6 The Industrial/Institutional Consumer

Read Section 2.6, **The Industrial/Institutional Consumer** (pages 74–76), in your textbook. In the space provided, summarize the key ideas and concepts discussed in this section, and then write two or three important things that you have learned.

Summary:

_____

_____

_____

_____

_____

_____

_____

_____

_____

_____

_____

_____

_____

_____

What have you learned in this section?

1. _____

_____

_____

_____

2. _____

_____

_____

_____

3. _____

_____

_____

_____

Matching

Draw a line from the type of need on the left to the slogan that appeals to this need on the right.

Physiological needs	"They melt in your mouth, not in your hand." (M&M's)
Safety needs	"The best a man can get." (Gillette)
Affiliation needs	"You're in good hands with Allstate." (Allstate Insurance)
Esteem needs	"A diamond is forever." (DeBeers)
Growth needs	"The Uncola." (7-Up)

Short Answer

1. Discuss how the state of the economy may affect the consumer demand for a new product. How do marketers adapt to fluctuations in the economy?

_____

_____

_____

_____

_____

_____

_____

_____

_____

_____

_____

_____

_____

_____

2. Draw a graph of the following nontraditional product life cycles: fad, niche, seasonal.

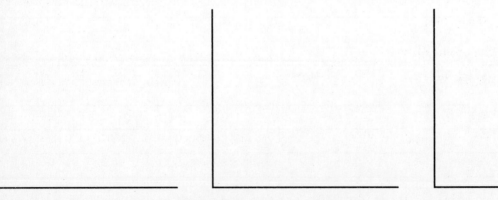

Word Search

Use the clues below to find out what the words are. Then find the words in the following puzzle.

```
B W P R O F I L E S U W S T O Q F D T I K B
A R T S W S Q S P F I R Q U P D E E S C O O
R L O D S D D E P A E D S U K A A M C V B R
R V D N D R E D O M O F H R M W O O L L M S
I U H E K T E U O I S C I H P A R G O E G I
E K H R R F R O K L L G P D J R Z R W C C Y
R L S T L F B T L Y L G L D E W I A M U U W
S B T O W Y E R J L C L S S R C U P V D E M
T U R M B O K R G I O O C C K U L H U R S E
O Y R A U D R D F F N I I S U M N I Y R C N
E I B V J S I G R E S T H D N S S C N C P T
N N B B A S L A D C I R P E R T T S T E E N
T G G I L Y K T E Y G F A D S H N O M Q E O
R P E N L U M E E C N M R U I C A R M T R I
Y R D D O K J K S L M D G J J S W S G E P T
Q O Q U W J I E W E E O O Y K Y M G R S R A
R C L S A D K E A Y N Y H Q N A E D S Y E V
T E T T N T L P N T T S C W Y G G U N H S I
I S S R C T K E S E N W Y E K R S S M N S T
L S O I E E L R F R E U S R P N I C H E U O
M H R A M D O A W R O D P E W E E D C H R M
T J F L N S S W O Q P N S Z R L N E T F E Z
```

Clues (with textbook page numbers)

The most important group to most businesses _____ (2 words) (55)

Manufacturers may pay a shelf _____ to retailers. (43)

The stage when sales of a product increase is the _____ stage. (43)

When sales decrease, the product is in its _____ stage. (45)

Factors preventing competitors from realizing a profit _____ (3 words) (44)

The person who buys a product _____ (37)

A person who makes a buying decision for someone else _____ (37)

Products we desire are _____. Products we must have are _____. (38)

Products that can be returned to manufacturers if they don't sell are on a _____ deal. (42)

Products that have a brief period of popularity are _____. Products that have a more lasting effect are _____. (47)

Consumer characteristics such as age, gender, and income level are _____. (51)

A system for measuring consumers' beliefs, opinions, and interests _____ (59)

The consideration of how wants and needs are effected by location _____ (60)

The forces that activate and direct behaviour _____ (67)

Social forces that motivate _____ (2 words) (68)

He developed the Law of Effect _____ (69)

A small section of the market is a _____. (48)

He modified Maslow's theory _____ (70)

According to Maslow, the need to be free of danger is the _____ and security need. (69)

The six steps to making a buying decision is called the _____. (2 words) (71)

Consumer _____ are descriptions of the kind of people that will be attracted to your product. (50)

Together, the stages of a consumer's life is called the _____. (3 words) (56)

_____/institutional consumer bases a buying decision on the needs of the organization. (74)

Multiple Choice

Circle the best response.

1. A customer is
   a) someone who buys a product
   b) always the consumer
   c) anyone who goes into a store
   d) anyone who reads an advertisement

2. The maturity stage in the product life cycle is the period in which sales
   a) decline
   b) increase
   c) stabilize
   d) end

3. Allowance customers
   a) have a double primary market
   b) still rely on gatekeepers for all purchases
   c) make purchase decisions that become habitual
   d) are beginning to make some purchasing decisions

4. Which motivational theorist would state that consumers are motivated to buy products that produce positive events and avoid products that produce negative events?
   a) Thorndike
   b) Maslow
   c) Alderfer
   d) Jung

P. Marketing Plan: The Consumer

Read page 80 in your textbook, **Marketing Plan**. Then work through the following to build on the marketing plan you started in Chapter 1.

Consumer Profile

General description of your target market:

_____

_____

_____

Specific description of your target market (fill in as much of this chart as possible):

Demographics	Psychographics	Geographics	Product Use Statistics	Product Life Cycle
gender:	beliefs:	urban:	heavy user:	traditional:
income:	attitudes:	suburban:	medium user:	fad:
social class:	lifestyle:	rural:	light user:	niche:
family life cycle:	religious beliefs:		non-user:	seasonal:
ethnicity and culture:	opinions:			

Consumer Demand Analysis

Complete an analysis of key economic and environmental indicators that will give you a better picture of the present economic climate.

Time Period	Unemployment Rate	Inflation	Interest Rates *(1 year variable rate)*	Canadian Exchange Rate	Prosperity or Recession
last year					
now					
future					

CHAPTER 3: The Competitive Market

A. Understanding Key Terms: Chapter Introduction

Before reading this chapter, write what you think each term means in the middle column of this chart. After reading this chapter, complete the column on the right. How do your definitions and the textbook's compare?

Term	What Do You Think It Means?	Definition from Text
free market		
profit		
perfect competition		
monopolistic competition		
oligopoly		
monopoly		
research and development		
direct competition		
indirect competition		
relationship marketing		
competitive market		
market share		
market segment		

B. Understanding the Ideas: 3.1 Competition in a Free Market

As you read Section 3.1, **Competition in a Free Market** (pages 83–88), in your textbook, fill in the charts below.

	Four Major Market Structures			
	#1 _____	#2 _____	#3 _____	#4 _____
Characteristics				

The Benefits of Competition

Benefit	Description of the benefit and why it comes about

Types of Competition

	Two Types of Competition	
	#1 _____	#2 _____
Characteristics		

C. Predicting Effects: Market Structures

Identify the type of market structure under which each of the following products and services competes. In the last column, describe how changes in the competitive environment might affect the type of products and services. The first row has been done for you as an example.

Original Circumstances	Market Structure	Redefined Circumstances	Effect of New Competition on the Product/Service
a single airline providing all domestic service	monopoly	four new airlines open for domestic flights	oligopoly—more competitive prices, more need for marketing
all retail stores (including grocery stores) are government owned and operated		an unregulated number of small retailers	
a handful of office productivity software producers, each with substantial market control		a large number of small producers of office productivity software, each with a degree of market control	
a single government owned and operated electricity provider		an unregulated number of small electricity distributors, each with an opportunity for some market control	
numerous unregulated privately owned skateboard parks, each with an opportunity for some market control		a single city owned and operated skateboard park	
Choose your own:			

D. Comparing Examples: Direct and Indirect Competition

In the chart below, list all the direct and indirect competitors for each of the following.

Business	Direct Competitors	Indirect Competitors
toothpaste		
a particular model of car (choose one) _____		
a retail outlet (choose one) _____		
a CD shop		
mobile phone service		
a credit card		

Complete the boxes below as you read Section 3.2, **Competitive Advantages** (pages 89–97), in your textbook.

Sustainable Competitive Advantages are _____ .

Non-Sustainable Competitive Advantages are _____ .

These include:

↓

Developing a unique selling proposition, which means _____
_____

These include:

↓

_____
_____
_____

_____
_____
_____

_____
_____
_____

_____
_____
_____

_____
_____
_____

_____
_____
_____

_____
_____
_____

What have you learned in this section? _____
_____
_____

F. Charting Examples: Sustainable Competitive Advantage

Provide a specific example for each of the products below and fill in the columns to show how a company might develop a sustainable competitive advantage for this product. Share your analysis with the class.

Product	Unique Selling Proposition (USP)	Is this product for a niche in the market? Explain.	From 1 to 10 (10 being very important), how important is customer loyalty in this industry? How could you create this?
a video game console _____ _____			
make–up _____ _____			
a brand of computer _____ _____			
a fast–food outlet _____ _____			
a hair salon or spa _____ _____			
a pair of athletic shoes _____ _____			
choose your own product _____ _____ _____			

G. Making Connections: Unique Selling Proposition (USP)

In the 1990s, management guru Tom Peters coined the phrase, "Brand YOU." According to Peters, as individuals in the world of work, you have to "become distinct or extinct." In the space below, explore how you might market yourself as a brand. What is your competitive advantage? What is your unique selling proposition (USP)? What qualities, characteristics, skills, attitudes, experiences, and so on set you apart? Reread page 89 in your textbook and ask yourself a similar question—Why would my target customer buy Brand Me instead of Competitor ABC?—and then go through the "if-then" scenarios.

(Hint: If you find this assignment difficult, you may seek the help of friends and family since they may be more aware of your strengths).

Brand ME

With a partner, choose a product you are familiar with. Imagine that the manufacturer of this product has hired the two of you to create a marketing strategy to increase the sales of their product. Your strategy should consider all of the non-sustainable competitive advantages listed below. Present your product and strategy to the class.

Product description: _____

_____

_____

_____

Promotion: _____

_____

_____

_____

Placement: _____

_____

_____

_____

Quality: _____

_____

_____

_____

Benefits of use: _____

_____

_____

_____

Price: _____

_____

_____

_____

Design features: _____

_____

_____

_____

I. Understanding the Ideas:
3.3 Service Competition and 3.4 The Product/Service Mix

Complete the following as you read Section 3.3, **Service Competition** (pages 99–104), and Section 3.4, **The Product/Service Mix** (pages 106–107), in your textbook.

Services are _____

Retail and wholesalers are _____

How are the two business categories alike? _____

_____

How are they different? _____

_____

Name and describe the service competition factors in the graphic below.

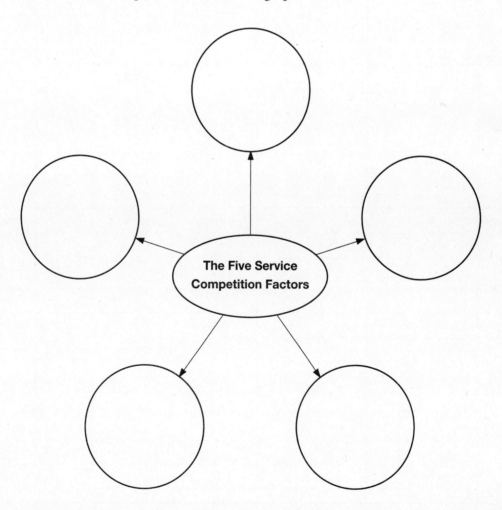

The Five Service Competition Factors

J. Rating and Creating Strategies: Service Competition and The Product/Service Mix

From 1 to 5 (5 being very important), rate how important you think each of the different elements of service competition is to each of the following. Explain how each of these services might use the different elements to set itself apart from its direct competitors.

	Convenience	Degree of Service	Selection	Reputation	Price
doctor/ doctor office					
hairstylist/ hair salon					
shoe store					
grocery store					
mechanic/ garage					

Complete the following as you read Section 3.5, **The Competitive Market** (pages 107–111), in your textbook.

The competitive market consists of _____

_____

Market share is _____

_____

A market segment is _____

_____

Two ways of increasing market share are (describe these):

A shift in share points informs the marketing manager that either (provide examples):

What have you learned in this section? _____

_____

_____

L. Analyzing Graphs: The Competitive Market

Study the table below and the bar graph on page 53, and then answer the questions that follow each.

The Canadian Soft Drink Market: Sales Volume & Per Capita Consumption by Region

Sales Volume & Per Capita Consumption by Region					
Region	Consumption (kL)	% Change vs 1999	Population July 1, 2000	2000 Per Capita Consumption	1999 Per Capita Consumption
Canada	3 472 056	-2.4%	30 750 100	112.9	116.4
Atlantic	328 400	-3.1%	2 375 300	138.3	142.7
Quebec	766 829	-3.5%	7 372 500	104.0	108.0
Ontario	1 319 790	-3.2%	11 670 300	113.1	118.0
West	1 057 037	-0.2%	9 333 000	113.3	114.3

Source: Population Statistics, Statistics Canada

1. What percentage of the Canadian beverage market does each of the geographical areas have?

   Atlantic: _____

   Quebec: _____

   Ontario: _____

   West: _____

2. List reasons why you think the consumption of soft drinks has declined.

   _____

   _____

   _____

   _____

   _____

   _____

   _____

   _____

   _____

   _____

   _____

   _____

   _____

   _____

   _____

   _____

Top 30 Countries—Soft Drink Consumption

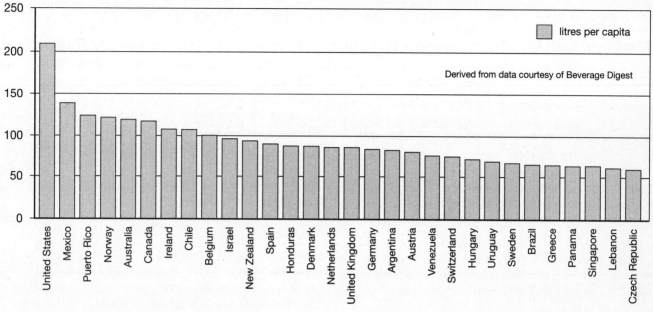

Notes:

* Based on 1998 per capita consumption data.

* Statistics are based on estimated total soft drink industry sales of traditional flavoured, carbonated soft drink beverages (e.g., colas, lemon-limes, ginger-ales, root beers, etc.) and does not include "new-age" beverages.

* Per capita consumption estimates were derived from data courtesy of *Beverage Digest*.

3. What does per capita mean?_____

_____

4. Based on the above graph, complete the following chart to calculate the approximate total consumption of soft drinks in each country. You can find the population for each country on the Internet.

Country	Approximate Number of Litres Per Capita	Country Population	Total Consumption for Country
United States			
Mexico			
Puerto Rico			
Norway			
Australia			
Canada			

5. Why is this useful information for soft drink marketers? _____

_____

_____

Read the article and answer the questions that follow.

Falling Profits Tarnish Golden Arches

By Jennifer Wells

YUM. I can just picture it. The dyspeptic teen approaches the counter, stares balefully at the customer who stands before him, and intones: "Will that be a sisal carpet with your Chicken Select Strips?"

What madness now, you ask?

Only the latest news out of McDonald's Corp. The burger chain—"over 99 billion served"—is so desperate to raise its sagging fortunes that it is considering selling other stuff besides food stuff at its restaurants.

The company, spokesperson Walt Riker said yesterday, is "looking at concepts that might go beyond restaurants, which could involve retail extension. "Riker did not specify what those extensions might be. Patty flippers? K-Tel stackers? Fluffy bathrobes?

It hurts the brain.

Why ever would McDonald's stray from its mainstay business?

Listen to Jack Greenberg and you'll get a quick taste of the company's woes. Greenberg is the corporation's chief executive officer, surely an unhappy task. Last week, from the company headquarters at One McDonald's Plaza in Oak Brook, Ill., the unfortunate Greenberg acknowledged that the year 2001 was the "most challenging" in the chain's history. Earnings are sagging. Net income last year fell to $1.6 billion (U.S.) from $2 billion the year previous. This year the trend continues, with profit for the first quarter falling more than 30 per cent to $253 million.

There's little point in trying to put a positive spin on those numbers, as some company supporters tried to do. To wit: If you pare away all the bad news, the company actually earned 31 cents a share in the three months ended March 31.

It's the bad news we need to scrutinize. Closing 32 "underperforming" restaurants in Turkey. That's one point to consider. Or asset impairment charges related to more under-performing outlets in Chile and Latin America.

What the company calls "systemwide sales"—sales from company restaurants and revenues from franchised and affiliated outlets—were down in Latin America, and down in the Asia/Pacific, Middle East, and Africa Group.

Sales were up 2 per cent in the U.S., thanks to new store openings, but down in Canada, slipping by $11 million to $320 million.

How come? Because we're all going to Tim Hortons, and submarine sandwich shops, that's how come.

It has been years, no exaggeration, since my own kids lobbied for a trip to the golden arches.

Two nights ago I asked the 10-year-old why this was. This is what he said: "It's sort of like false advertising. The Big Macs look big and juicy in the pictures, but really they're not." Also: "It's bad for you." And: "I think some of the foods are real. I think the pickles are real, and maybe the ketchup and the mustard."

McDonald's has been struggling for years—all right, for-ever —with the perception that its offerings aren't "real." It has been a losing battle thus far. Introducing the "Made for You" preparation system through Canada, U.S., and a third of the Japanese outlets was meant to evoke more the feel of made-to-order and less the feel of assembly line. But the $162 million just-in-time experiment failed to woo con-sumers, who perhaps were unimpressed with the company's pledge that each sandwich is "assembled to order."

To offset its burger difficulties, McDonald's inhouse has reached for such breakthrough fare as the aforementioned "Chicken Select Strips"—all white meat, lightly breaded chicken fingers in "adult-sized" portions—and externally in the U.S. to alliances with such non-burger chains as Chipotle (burritos) and Donatos (pizza). The latter move, says the company, is a way to capture "additional meal occasions."

Last month, it announced the opening of its first "town centre" restaurant, in suburban Columbus, Ohio. The centre, said the company in a statement, includes a "first-of-its kind interactive miniature drive-thru for kids, a karaoke booth for customers to record CDs, and a separate area for adults to eat and gather."

McDonald's had little to say about what these adults would actually be eating there—though it did trumpet "Lavazza coffee from Italy"—nor what, gastronomically, would appeal to the Tween market, which it surely hopes to win over with the recording artist idea. And, no, it didn't explain what an "interactive miniature drive-thru" is.

In Japan the company is touting a deal struck with Softbank Corp. to offer high-speed internet kiosks in as many as 4000 Mickey D's in that country. But Starbucks Coffee Japan Ltd. has reached a similar arrangement, an alliance that lends itself more obviously to internet cafes.

Perhaps it was only inevitable that growth for McDonald's would be sought outside the food arena.

McDonald's own food offerings seem to bring it nothing but bad PR, from the company's admission that, well, yes, there is beef fat in those hot oil vats into which vast quantities of french fries are sunk, to recent advertorials running in some French magazines advising that children shouldn't eat at McDonald's more than once a week. (The ads were placed by the French arm of the McDonald's empire and were meant to make the point that the fast–food chain is nutritionally conscious, too. Instead, the suggestion that children's meals should be devised "in relation to his weight and physical activities" only makes the point that, nutritionally speaking, McDonald's shouldn't even be an option. Here's a funny coincidence: Happy Meals were introduced in 1979 and children's obesity rates started to climb the following year.)

McDonald's customers aren't happy. A recent article in *Fortune* magazine reported that the University of Michigan's American Customer Satisfaction index has rated McDonald's dead last every year in the past decade, which is as long as the survey has been in existence. Jack Greenberg could have fixed that. Instead, he thinks that selling, who knows, screwdrivers will do the trick.

To which one can only say, Good McLuck.

Source: The Toronto Star, *May 30, 2002, pages D1 and D13.*

1. Why is McDonald's pursuing the idea of diversifying its product line?

_____

_____

_____

_____

2. According to the article, why are young people not as loyal to McDonald's as they once were?

_____

_____

_____

_____

3. Where are customers going for their fast food in Canada? Does this suggest a shift in consumer tastes, or a shift in the competition within the market segment?

_____

_____

_____

_____

4. Discuss McDonald's' attempt to capture "additional meal occasions." What is the strategic advantage of this? What might the effect of this move be on McDonald's market share? Has any other fast–food chain attempted this?

_____

_____

_____

_____

5. In terms of maintaining or growing market share, explore some reasons why McDonald's
    would introduce the following.

    "Made for You" Preparation: _____

    _____

    Town centres: _____

    _____

    Chicken Select Strips: _____

    _____

    McPizza: _____

    _____

    Interactive miniature drive-thrus: _____

    _____

    Karaoke booths: _____

    _____

    Internet connections: _____

    _____

6. The text suggests that to grow market share a company has to either increase the market
    size or take sales away from the competition. Discuss how McDonald's has attempted both
    of these strategies.

    _____

    _____

    _____

    _____

    _____

    _____

    _____

    _____

7. If you were running the McDonald's empire, what would you do to stay competitive with the
    fast–food industry while trying to please customers and critics of your food?

    _____

    _____

    _____

    _____

    _____

    _____

    _____

N. Understanding the Ideas:
3.6 Competing in International Markets

Fill in the following chart as you read Section 3.6, **Competing in International Markets** (pages 113–117), in your textbook.

Market Strategy Element	Challenges
promotion	
placement	
quality	
benefits of use	
pricing	
design	

What have you learned in this section? _____

_____

_____

Read this case study and then answer the questions that follow.

The Doughnut Wars

Tim Hortons has dominated the long-standing battle for market-share in Canada's coffee and doughnut industry. Started in a small shop over 36 years ago by professional hockey player Tim Horton and Hamilton ex-cop Ron Joyce, this company now sells over three million doughnuts *every day!* In 1999 Tim Hortons out-earned its closest competitor, Second Cup, by more than $1.26 billion. The company has expanded its menu offerings selling items like muffins, cakes, pies, croissants, soups, and chili. In 1995, this expansion continued as Tim Hortons merged with Wendy's International Inc., providing a new focus for expansion into the United States. Tim Hortons now has more than 120 outlets in six states.

But while Tim Hortons has made its move southward, a new US competitor has moved up north. Krispy Kreme Donuts, founded in 1937, has become a leading branded specialty retailer in the US. It produces more than 5 million doughnuts every day (1.8 billion per year) in its 192 stores across 31 states. It now plans on establishing a foothold in Canada by opening over 30 Canadian outlets. Though the number of outlets is small compared to Tim Hortons 2000+ outlets in Canada, Krispy Kreme's reputation for a high quality product, an aggressive distribution strategy, and a unique production process has its Canadian competitors a little nervous.

Joyce built a success formula for Tim Hortons by focusing on "Always Fresh" products and outstanding service. But Krispy Kreme has brought a new twist to this. When customers walk into a Krispy Kreme outlet, they can watch a fully automated production process that produces up to 250 dozen doughnuts an hour. And watch they do. When a new batch of its flagship doughnut, the "Krispy Kreme Original Glazed," is ready, the store announces it to its customers with the unique glowing red "HOT DONUTS NOW" sign. But these unique features are only a small concern to competitors compared to the product that these machines produce. "Delicious, mouth watering, to die for, and hot!" is how some would describe a Krispy Kreme doughnut. Even three months after opening its doors at its first Canadian location in Mississauga, Ontario, people were still lining up to buy a doughnut that costs 25% more than any other competition!

Krispy Kreme's aggressive placement strategy is also of concern. In addition to its stores, Krispy Kreme's premium quality doughnuts are sold in supermarkets, convenience stores, and other retail outlets throughout the United States. This not only opens up a larger market, it makes Krispy Kreme a household name. Such a strategy is not foreign to the people at Tim Hortons. The large number of Tim Hortons outlets is meant to generate brand recognition and to "train" the customer to visit the store several times a day.

It will be interesting to see if Krispy Kreme will have a lasting effect on the Canadian doughnut market. It has some real obstacles to overcome. Though his name is fading into history, Tim Horton will always have the legacy of once being a Canadian hockey hero. And even though it is now part of a US conglomerate, Tim Hortons will always have its Canadian roots. It will also be interesting to watch how Tim Hortons reacts to this new challenge. The size of its response will be telling of how significant it feels the Krispy Kreme threat is.

1. What seems to be Krispy Kreme's international marketing strategy?

	Krispy Kreme's Marketing Strategy
promotion	
placement	
quality	
benefits of use	
pricing	
design	

2. What element of the marketing strategy do Tim Hortons and Krispy Kreme seem to be emphasizing? You may want to visit each company's Web site (www.timhortons.com and www.krispykreme.com) to see what their marketing message focuses on.

_____

_____

_____

_____

_____

_____

_____

_____

_____

3. When you visit either a Tim Hortons store or its Web site, is it apparent how it is attempting to counter the Krispy Kreme threat?

_____

_____

_____

_____

_____

_____

_____

_____

_____

_____

4. What obstacles will Krispy Kreme face with its introduction into Canada? What challenges does Tim Hortons face in the United States?

_____

_____

_____

_____

_____

_____

_____

_____

_____

_____

Crossword

Use the clues below to solve this puzzle.

Across

1. This type of competition has products that are closely related.

4. The percentage that a company's product takes of the total dollars spent in that specific market (2 words)

6. A sales promotion method

9. The largest single market in the world

13. If two products or services are similar, this is usually the deciding factor.

14. A type of market structure with a few large companies each having market control

15. This factor drives business

16. Canadians live in this type of market economy. (2 words)

17. A type of market structure with a single company having complete market control

18. A market structure where many companies have market control (2 words)

Down

2. This encourages the creation of new businesses

3. The market is broken down into these smaller categories. (2 words)

5. A market structure where a large number of small companies has no opportunity for market control (2 words)

6. This company owns and operates many restaurants. (2 words)

7. Taxes placed on goods imported into a country

8. Canada's partnerships with foreign countries (2 words)

10. This occurs when a consumer thinks of one brand before any other. (4 words)

11. Word of mouth can help or hinder this for a company.

12. One of the major reasons why people shop on the Internet

Matching

Draw a line from the strategy on the left to the non-sustainable competitive advantage on the right.

"roll up the rim to win"   price

"Gucci Gloves"   benefits of use

"Volkswagen Beetle looks different from a Mustang"   design features

"selling Seaman's in Vancouver"   promotion

"automobiles offering greater safety"   quality

"Lamborghini coming up with an economy car"   placement

Fill in the Blanks

1. _____ contributes to the Canadian economy by encouraging the creation of new businesses.

2. Companies encourage their employees by being innovative in their _____ department.

3. If a company manages to attract more and more customers to their particular product, thus resulting in more _____, they also gain a bigger _____ of the market.

4. Retail and wholesale businesses are considered part of the _____ sector.

Q. Marketing Plan: The Competitive Market

Read page 120 in your textbook, **Marketing Plan**. Using the product, service, idea, or cause you chose for your marketing plan in the previous chapters, complete the following questions to help you extend your plan.

1. List as many direct competitors for your product, service, idea, or cause. _____

    _____

    _____

2. Using the chart below, create a competitive analysis by selecting at least three (3) direct competitors from your list in question 1 above.

	Your Product, Service, Idea, or Cause	Direct Competitor #1	Direct Competitor #2	Direct Competitor #3
Sustainable Advantages				
unique selling proposition				
production costs				
niche market				
customer loyalty and how to achieve it				
Non-Sustainable Advantages				
promotion				
placement				
quality				
benefit of use				
price				
design feature				

3. Since your product, service, idea, or cause will be in the introductory stage, what can you do to start increasing your market share?

_____

_____

_____

_____

_____

_____

_____

_____

_____

_____

_____

_____

CHAPTER 4: Marketing Research

A. Understanding Key Terms: Chapter Introduction

Before reading this chapter, write what you think each term means in the middle column of this chart. After reading this chapter, complete the column on the right. How do your definitions and the textbook's compare?

Term	What Do You Think It Means?	Definition from Text
marketing research		
hard data		
secondary data		
primary research		
qualitative research		
test market		
survey		
observation		
focus group		
consumer research		
product research		
margin of error		

B. Understanding the Ideas: 4.1 What Is Marketing Research?

As you read Section 4.1, **What Is Marketing Research?** (pages 123–125), in your textbook, fill in the information below to create a study tool.

Two Types of Information on Which Decisions Can Be Made	
Marketing research is...	*Intuitive decision is...*

Two examples of when marketing research is needed are:

1. _____

2. _____

A business could use this information to make decisions such as:

1. _____

2. _____

3. _____

Marketing research firms provide businesses with_____

_____

_____

They work with two types of data: _____ and _____

What have you learned in this section?_____

_____

_____

_____

_____

_____

C. Understanding the Ideas: 4.2 Gathering Secondary Data

As you read Section 4.2, **Gathering Secondary Data** (pages 127–132), in your textbook, fill in the information below to create a study tool.

Secondary data is _____

_____

Secondary research involves _____

_____

Its value is limited because _____

It is still used because _____

Secondary Source	Description	Example from Textbook

An example of how a business might use secondary data is _____

_____

What have you learned in this section? _____

_____

Read this article and answer the questions that follow.

Census as Secondary Market Research

The fact that new census figures are out won't surprise Canadians—most will remember filling out the eighteen-page census form in 2001. But what may surprise people is how all of that information is being used. Yes, the information does perform its original functions, such as allowing the government to realign electoral boundaries and enabling school boards to project enrolments. But this information is also central to many of the business decisions made across Canada each year.

The census-takers have, in effect, achieved what no private company could ever afford to do. They have created a neighbourhood-by-neighbourhood snapshot of the age, sex, population, marital status, living arrangements, housing, language, mobility, citizenship, ethnic background, employment, transportation to work, education, earnings, income, and religion of the Canadian population. Those statistics lie at the core of any business' marketing plan, and also inform any plans for existing companies to relocate or expand.

For the first time this year, Statistics Canada is making most of the census data available free of charge on the Internet. But the information that is posted here is available only at the municipality level. This is fine if someone just wants to know how many women, Chinese-Canadians, married couples, or people who work in management live in a particular two-block area. That information is readily available. But this in itself has limited value to businesses. The true value of the census information is only realized when businesses are able to zoom in closer and begin to "cross" the statistics. But for this they have to pay.

For a profile of a dissemination area, Statistics Canada's most microscopic level of 400 to 700 people on average, the cost starts at about $65. Though this level of detail is more helpful than the information provided in the above example, the richness of the census data only begins to emerge when these statistics are crossed. For instance, for the example given above, cross-tabulation would enable a business to see how many of the women in that two-block area are of Chinese descent, between the ages of 20–24, married, and professionally employed in management! The starting price for this kind of cross-tabulation is about $1000.

Firms can also order detailed demographic profiles and tabulations of business areas, since that's where their customers likely spend more of their time, says Jim McKibbin of Statistics Canada. Most will run up bills into the $10 000-range, requesting an updated picture of their specific target market in pockets across the country as each new layer of data is released. But those fees don't go toward the colossal $412.5 million cost of collecting and processing the census figures. The government picks up the $34.75 per household cost. "The fees paid by businesses," says McKibbin, "are intended only to cover the cost of consultation and manipulating the data."

With the basics provided, a company will combine its own research and other indexes to conclude not only how much money the local population has, but also what they generally spend it on. "Census information is the starting point for analysis of the market you are in or want to expand into," says Chris Michels, product manager for data at MapInfo Canada. "You'll look at the population of the area, and stock your store accordingly. An older area will have a different product mix than a younger area."

It's not unwittingly that the government does this kind of legwork for businesses. They consult with them, among other stakeholders, in formulating the 59 questions asked. The result is a treasure trove of information for most businesses across the country. They use the information for many things, the most obvious to draw the initial lines on their marketing plans. As Ken Jones, director of the Centre for the Study of Commercial Activity at Ryerson Polytechnic University points out, "If you want to understand your market, the census is your fundamental source."

Source: Adapted from "Selling the census" by Catherine Porter, The Toronto Star, July 14, 2002, pages C1 and C5.

1. What was the census originally used for? _____

   _____

   _____

   _____

   _____

   _____

2. What kind of information does the most recent census provide? _____

   _____

   _____

   _____

   _____

   _____

3. What limitations are there on the information that is available on the Internet, free of charge? _____

   _____

   _____

   _____

   _____

   _____

4. Do you think the information that is provided free has any use to a small start-up business? Why or why not? _____

   _____

   _____

   _____

   _____

   _____

5. Do you think the government should charge more, less, or no charge for this information? Explain your answer. Be sure to consider the effects on both small and large businesses. _____

   _____

   _____

   _____

   _____

   _____

   _____

As you read Section 4.3, **Gathering Primary Data** (pages 134–143), in your textbook, fill in the information below to create a study tool.

Primary data is _____

_____

Two types of primary research are:

1. _____, which is _____

2. _____, which is _____

Five Techniques of Primary Research	Description	How the Gathering Process May Work	Example

F. Creating a Survey: Gathering Primary Data

You and your partners have been hired by a well-finance start-up company to do market research. One of the ways you have decided on to collect information is to do a survey.

1. Alone, with a partner, or as a group, decide on the kind of start-up company that has hired you and then design a 10-question market research survey.

    Description of the company: _____

    _____

    _____

    _____

2. The following are some of the things to consider when setting up your survey:
    - Who are its intended customers? What is their age group?
    - What are their customer's needs?
    - What can their customers afford?
    - What kind of location would be best for the company?

    Then use the space below to write your questions. Be sure that you balance your questions and make use of the variety of questioning techniques you learned in the chapter.

    _____

    _____

    _____

    _____

    _____

    _____

    _____

    _____

    _____

    _____

    _____

    _____

    _____

    _____

    _____

    _____

    _____

    _____

3. Once you have created the questions, make recommendations about how the survey should be conducted.

   - Where should it be conducted?
   - When should it be conducted?
   - How is this information to be collected?

   Recommendations for conducting the survey: _____

   _____

   _____

   _____

   _____

   _____

   _____

   _____

   _____

4. Describe how you and your partner(s) will use at least two other sources of primary data to support your survey findings.

   _____

   _____

   _____

   _____

   _____

   _____

   _____

   _____

   _____

   _____

   _____

   _____

   _____

   _____

   _____

   _____

   _____

G. Understanding the Ideas: 4.4 Types of Marketing Research

While reading Section 4.4, **Types of Marketing Research** (pages 145–154), in your textbook, complete the following information.

Consumer research consists of _____

_____

_____

_____

_____

Competitive research is _____

_____

_____

_____

_____

1. _____

_____

Example: _____

2. _____

_____

Example: _____

3. _____

_____

Example: _____

4. _____

_____

Example: _____

1. _____

_____

Example: _____

2. _____

_____

Example: _____

3. _____

_____

Example: _____

4. _____

_____

Example: _____

5. _____

_____

Example: _____

6. _____

_____

Example: _____

7. _____

_____

Example: _____

8. _____

_____

Example: _____

9. _____

_____

Example: _____

In the chart below, provide an example of how you might use primary and secondary research to collect information about the consumer and competitive markets.

	Type of Marketing Research	Primary Research	Secondary Research
Consumer Research	awareness		
	attitudes		
	usage		
	consumer segmentation analysis		
	market dimension analysis		
	product research		
	media research		
	consumer-tracking devices		
	motivation research		

	Type of Marketing Research	Primary Research	Secondary Research
	consumer satisfaction studies		
	advertising research		
Competitive Research	competitive market analysis		
	competitive intelligence		
	pricing research		
	conjoint (tradeoff) analysis		

I. Matching Concepts: Types of Marketing Research

Draw a line from each marketing research type on the left to its description on the right.

advertising research   "a psychological perspective into buying behaviour"

market dimension analysis   "provides information on how to effectively convey product message"

motivation research   "group potential customers into target markets"

consumer segmentation analysis   "segment consumers based on what they read, watch, or hear"

media research   "researches the main issues that influence a consumer segment"

As you read Section 4.5, **Preparing the Research Report** (pages 155–159), in your textbook, fill in the following outline to create a study tool.

Preparing the Research Report

A. Statement of _____

B. Review of the _____

    i. A _____ of _____

    ii. I_____ of _____

    iii. S _____ of _____

What have you learned in this section?_____

_____

_____

_____

_____

_____

_____

_____

_____

K. Analyzing Marketing Research Data: Mean, Mode, and Median

When conducting marketing research, one way to analyze the data is to calculate the mean, mode, and/or median of a group of numbers to compare results.

Mean is the average of a list of numbers. It is calculated by adding the list and dividing it by the total number of numbers.

Mode is the number that occurs the most number of times in the list of numbers.

Median is calculated by listing all the numbers in numerical order from smallest to largest and determining the middle number in the group. If there is an even number, then the mean (average) of the two middle numbers is the median.

Advertising Agencies Salaries

Title	Starting Salary ($000s)	Top Salary ($000s)
1. President/CEO	200	700
2. Director of Client Services/Managing Director	125	275
3. Group Account Director	90	180
4. Account Director	80	120
5. Account Supervisor	45	80
6. Account Executive	25	60
7. Creative Director	150	600
8. Copywriter	25	250
9. Art Director	25	250
10. Account Planner/Strategic Planner	30	225
11. Media Director	85	250
12. Media Planner	20	120
13. Media Buyer	20	90

Source: http://www.marketingmag.ca/index.cgi

Using the definitions and the chart above, calculate the following:

	Starting Salary ($000s)	Top Salary ($000s)
Mean		
Mode		
Median		

L. Representing Marketing Research Data: Graphing

Graphing is an effective way to communicate. It is clear, concise, easy to interpret and understand, and a great visual method of learning. The purpose is to show a relationship and to illustrate trends. Although it may be costly and time-consuming to create, a chart can be a convincing, compact way to convey information.

There are three common types of graphs: line, bar, and circle (pie chart) graph. Look at the following two examples and answer the questions below each of them.

Pie Chart

Customer Base by Age Group—GenX Design Inc.

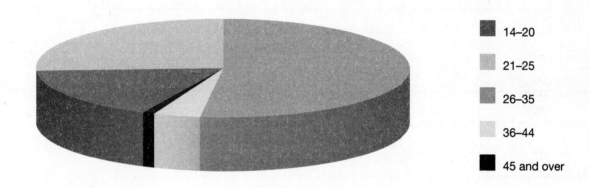

- 14–20
- 21–25
- 26–35
- 36–44
- 45 and over

1. Which age group represents about 50% of GenX Design's target market?

_____

_____

_____

_____

2. Which two age groups *together* represent almost 45% of GenX Design's target market?

_____

_____

_____

_____

3. Based on the information in this graph, what recommendations would you make to GenX Design with regard to its advertising and the "feel" of its stores? _____

_____

_____

_____

_____

_____

Line Graph

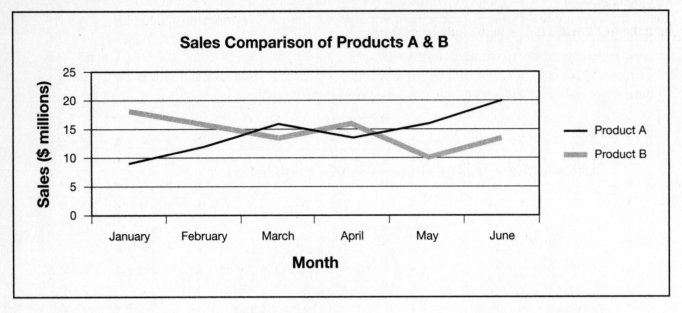

Sales Comparison of Products A & B

1. Which product saw an increase in sales in March?

   _____

   _____

2. What months were the sales for Product B higher than Product A?

   _____

   _____

3. Which product had sales of $20 million in June?

   _____

   _____

4. Can you think of reasons why Product B's sales started to decrease over the course of the first half of the year?

   _____

   _____

   _____

   _____

   _____

   _____

   _____

   _____

   _____

Word Search

Find the words listed below in the following puzzle.

```
C  S  T  A  T  Y  S  S  A  I  S  T  I  C  S  C  D  E  I  L  N  M
O  R  A  N  A  E  I  P  E  W  D  A  I  S  A  G  A  N  N  L  O  A
R  E  R  E  A  V  S  A  E  C  A  B  T  S  E  C  T  V  T  A  I  R
R  N  O  N  D  R  Y  T  A  R  O  R  I  R  Y  S  A  I  U  C  T  K
E  N  O  U  R  U  L  A  C  E  I  N  E  A  F  O  B  R  I  E  S  E
L  A  R  M  A  S  A  D  R  K  E  O  D  N  S  T  A  O  T  R  E  T
A  L  R  E  S  E  N  D  A  R  C  H  D  A  E  X  S  N  I  R  U  R
T  P  P  R  I  M  A  R  Y  D  A  T  A  I  R  S  E  I  V  E  Q  E
I  A  S  D  R  E  T  A  E  S  O  B  D  B  C  Y  S  C  E  T  D  S
O  I  E  E  T  W  N  H  V  D  C  F  U  J  G  A  D  S  I  F  E  E
N  D  W  W  E  V  I  T  A  T  I  T  N  A  U  Q  L  A  C  A  D  A
S  E  K  E  P  U  O  R  G  S  U  C  O  F  H  E  E  I  T  Y  N  R
S  M  B  K  Y  R  J  S  T  E  K  R  A  M  T  S  E  T  N  A  E  C
C  E  O  S  E  E  N  F  E  D  Q  U  E  N  T  I  O  N  R  D  N  H
U  F  W  O  D  N  O  I  T  A  T  N  E  M  G  E  S  E  Z  H  E  C
R  A  N  D  O  M  C  G  N  I  N  I  M  A  T  A  D  I  V  G  P  X
C  O  N  S  U  M  E  R  R  E  S  E  A  R  C  H  V  I  G  U  O  Z
D  E  T  A  L  L  O  C  L  I  S  T  S  E  R  V  S  Y  Q  B  F  P
```

awareness	Environics	primary data
bias	focus group	quantitative
collated	hard data	random
conjoint analysis	intuitive	secondary data
consumer research	listserv	segmentation
correlations	market research	skewed
databases	media planner	survey
data mining	open-ended question	test markets
day after recall	periodical index	

Hidden Message

With some of the unused letters, find the hidden message. (Hint: The message appears in the top seven lines of the puzzle. It contains ten words.)

Multiple Choice

Circle the best response.

1. Which of the following is NOT an example of secondary data?

   a) financial statements

   b) interviews

   c) trade magazines

   d) Statistics Canada

2. Primary data may be collected by which of the following methods?

   a) observation

   b) experimentation

   c) survey

   d) all of the above

3. The most complete, accurate, and expensive information would be gathered in a(n)

   _____ survey.

   a) observation

   b) personal interview

   c) mail

   d) telephone

4. Which Canadian city is often used as a test market?

   a) Whistler, British Columbia

   b) Montreal, Quebec

   c) Peterborough, Ontario

   d) Winnipeg, Manitoba

5. A relationship between holiday car accidents and drinking is known as

   a) collate

   b) correlation

   c) test market

   d) util

Fill in the Blanks

1. _____ is marketing-research information that has been collected and

   published by others. An example of this is _____.

2. _____ is unanalyzed, current information collected by a researcher for a

   specific purpose. An example is _____.

3. A small group of people, representative of a target market, who are brought together to discuss a

   product or problem is referred to as a _____.

4. Product research is about more than just developing a new product. Doing research to find new

   _____ for existing products can be just as important.

N. Marketing Plan: Marketing Research

Complete the following using your product, service, idea, or cause you have used in the previous chapters. You may wish to use page 162 in your textbook as an example.

Stage 1: Identify a marketing problem.

_____

_____

_____

_____

_____

_____

Stage 2: Determine what information you will need to help you solve this problem.

_____

_____

_____

_____

_____

Stage 3: Decide how the data will be collected. Could you use the census data in any way?

_____

_____

_____

_____

_____

Stage 4: Design a survey. What questions will you include? What is the format going to be?

_____

_____

_____

_____

_____

_____

_____

Stage 5: Interpret and analyze your results. (Use the space below.) You may wish to use graphs to illustrate some of your results.

CHAPTER 5: Product Development

A. Understanding Key Terms: Chapter Introduction

Before reading this chapter, write what you think each term means in the middle column of this chart. After reading this chapter, complete the column on the right. How do your definitions and the textbook's compare?

Term	What Do You Think It Means?	Definition from Text
benefit analysis		
feasibility study		
invention		
innovation		
prototype		
information utility		
place utility		
time utility		
market potential		
MOA (marketing opportunity analysis)		
test marketing		
product launch		

As you read Section 5.1, **Marketing and Product Development** (pages 165–168), in your textbook, fill in information about the product development process in the map below to create a study tool.

Informs efforts of

M_____ R_____ shows business people _____ _____.

Points to

P_____ & D_____ asks "_____ _____?"

This department estimates the cost of producing the product.

The marketing department uses the production data to

The M_____ department asks "_____ _____?"

Marketers continually feed _____ _____ to the _____.

Develops a prototype to test the product

Gathers feedback about the prototype and communicates it to Production & Design

P_____ D_____ Process
- must be done at start-up (example from textbook): ____
  _____
- is also done when new products are developed
  (example from textbook): _____
  _____

A company may also conduct a feasibility study to _____
_____
This leads to a final decision.

C. Charting the Concepts: Feasibility Study

A feasibility study is sometimes necessary to determine whether or not it is worthwhile pursuing a new product concept. Consider an existing product or service that you think would have required a feasibility study. What issues would have needed to be addressed in the study? What actions do you believe would be required to resolve these issues? What department would be responsible for completing the required tasks? Use the chart below to keep track of your answers.

Product or service: _____

Issue	Actions Required to Resolve This Issue	Responsibility

D. Understanding the Ideas: 5.2 Invention or Innovation?

As you read Section 5.2, **Invention or Innovation?** (pages 170–172), in your textbook, complete the following information to create a study tool.

Successful product development starts with an idea or concept based on _____

a _____ for the _____.

	Two Different Types of New Products	
	I_____	I_____
Definition		
Examples		

Identify two pieces of new information that you have learned in this section. What is the significance of each to marketing?

_____

_____

_____

_____

_____

_____

_____

_____

_____

_____

_____

_____

_____

_____

E. Classifying Products: Invention or Innovation?

In the chart below, classify each of the following products as an invention or innovation.

Industry	Product/Service	Invention/ Innovation	Rationale for Your Classification
Electronics	cell phones		
	DVDs		
	Palm™ Pilots		
	Your example:		
Fashion	reversible clothing		
	men's skincare products		
	Lycra® or Gortex®		
	Your example:		
Sporting Goods	snowboard		
	in-line skates		
	Nike shoes		
	Your example:		
Miscellaneous	On-Star Global Positioning Service		
	power bars		
	scented markers		
	Your example:		

F. Researching on the Internet: Inventions

According to a study in the *Journal of Product Innovation Management*, roughly 10 out of 11 new product ideas are not commercially successful. Robert McMath, a former marketer, has developed a "Museum of Flops" containing a collection of more than 65 000 items, of which a section is made up of "new product blunders" (as opposed to "new product wonders").

Search the Internet for sites and articles that discuss McMath's product flops and complete the following.

1. Identify three products that flopped and explain why you believe these products failed.

Brand Name	Product Description	Reasons for Failure

2. Identify at least three products that you can recall that are no longer on the market.

_____

_____

_____

3. Do you think the products you listed above were failures? Explain.

_____

_____

_____

4. What might some other reasons be for a manufacturer removing a product from the market?

_____

_____

_____

G. Understanding the Ideas:
5.3 The Stages of Product Development

As you read Section 5.3, **The Stages of Product Development** (pages 174–178), in your textbook, use the chart below to record the typical stages a company goes through before it can introduce a new product in the marketplace.

Stage	Description
1.	
2.	
3.	
4.	
5.	
6.	
7.	
8.	

Read the case study and then answer the questions that follow.

Footless, Bulge-Free and Rich to Boot: Turning a Simple Idea Into a Million-Dollar Business

Most entrepreneurs start their businesses in reaction to a perceived problem. In Sara Blakely's case, the problem was related to a personal fashion disaster. When trying on her new tight-fitting cream pants, Blakely was appalled to find that the material did not lie smoothly and the snug, light material accentuated aspects of her figure that she would rather hide. One day as she was watching the Oprah Winfrey show, she became aware that she was not alone in this experience. Winfrey spontaneously hiked up her pant-legs to show her amused audience that she had hacked the feet off her nylons in order to get the smooth look she wanted, while still having the "naked toes" demanded by summer footwear. This moment triggered the birth of Spanx in Sara Blakely's mind!

Blakely felt that she could produce and market "footless pantyhose." She started to research this possibility by visiting knitting mills and Georgia Tech to research patents. A negative response greeted Blakely at every turn, however. She learned that if there was a market for her product in the multi-billion dollar hosiery industry, the large companies would "cut her off at the feet" before she could establish her brand. Despite these warnings, Blakely felt that Winfrey's impromptu confession on national television was support enough for her idea.

Blakely was not a traditional businessperson by any stretch of the imagination. She did not go to business school, employ outside consultants, take a small business course, or borrow money from the bank to get started. The two things she did have was $50 000 that she borrowed from her grandmother and an unwavering belief that she had discovered a niche in an otherwise saturated market. As well, she had an individual sense of marketing on which she would base her branding efforts. Her intent was to address a serious need in the market while maintaining a fun and funky marketing approach.

For an example of her marketing approach, one need not look any further than the name of her product. Blakely developed the name Spanx because, as a comedian, she knew that "K" sounding words make people laugh! She brought this same unconventional approach to her sales effort. When making her first sales call to the department store Neiman Marcus, she did an actual demonstration wearing her cream pants without Spanx and then changed into the Spanx to show the dramatic difference. Neiman Marcus bought the untraditional approach and a sizable order as well. Bloomingdale's followed, and Blakely became a pro at her cold call strategy. After an appearance on the Oprah Winfrey show, Blakely sold $30 000 worth of Spanx in two days! Barbara Atkin, Holt Renfrew's fashion director says of Spanx "It's been a complete success," citing Spanx's bright red packaging with its cartoon insert as being particularly attractive. As Atkin put it, "Hoisery has always been so serious."

Blakely has made some errors along the way, but some of them were quite welcomed. For example, her sales prediction of $1.6 million for the first year was off by 25 percent—sales for the year were actually over the $2 million mark! These kinds of numbers brought rapid responses from larger manufacturers. Big-name companies quickly followed Blakely into this niche by producing copycat products of their own. Despite this, she does not appear overly concerned. At 31 years of age, she owns 100% of her multi-million dollar company, she is debt free, and has recently launched a new product.

Source: Adapted from Jennifer Wells "Footless, bulge-free and rich to boot: Turning a simple idea into a million-dollar business," The Toronto Star, May 25, 2002, pages D1 and D5.

1. As the case suggests, Sara Blakely is not a "traditional businessperson." It could be said that the Spanx success story is not traditional either. Map out the development of Spanx in relation to the product development stages, and then comment on how closely Blakely followed the product development model. Be sure to note the things that Blakely did well, as well as things that you think she could have done better.

Stage	Do you think Sara Blakely performed this stage well? Explain.
1.	
2.	
3.	
4.	
5.	
6.	
7.	
8.	

2. Earlier you read that 10 out of every 11 inventions are not viable. Based on your analysis of Blakely's performance at each of the product development stages above, would you say Spanx is lucky to have succeeded? Why did it succeed? Explain.

_____

_____

_____

_____

3. What is the main problem (threat) facing Spanx?

_____

_____

_____

_____

1. When inventors register an idea in Canada, they are legally protected against other companies copying and selling their ideas for 20 years. Do you think individuals or corporations should have the right to protect their ideas? Why or why not?

_____

_____

_____

_____

_____

_____

_____

_____

_____

_____

_____

_____

2. Do you think Sara Blakely's idea for footless hosiery should be protected? Why or why not?

_____

_____

_____

_____

_____

_____

_____

_____

_____

_____

_____

As you read Section 5.4, **Product Development and Utility** (pages 180–188), in your textbook, fill in the information below.

Utility is_____

Type of Utility	Explanation	Example
F_____ (see chart below)		
I_____		
P_____		
T_____		
P_____		

There are six important components to form utility. List these in the diagram below and explain each using an example.

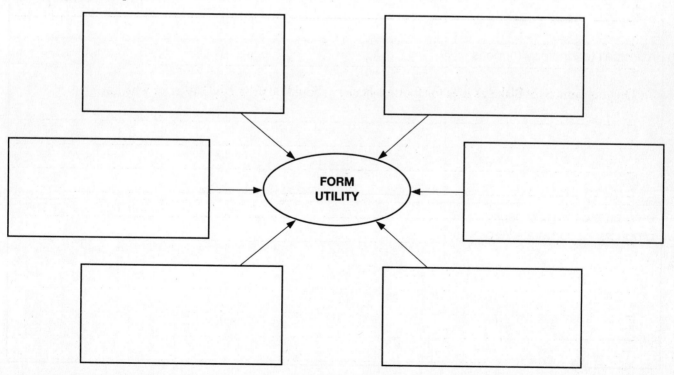

K. Identifying and Explaining Situations: Product Utility

For each of the following situations, identify and explain which utility is being represented.

Situation	Utility	Explanation
highway billboards that indicate the distance to and features of a local hotel		
twist-off milk carton caps		
exciting new colours used for computer hardware		
roller ball technology for pens		
e-commerce (e.g., ordering products via corporate Web sites)		

L. Understanding the Ideas:
5.5 Product Development and the Marketing Concept

Read Section 5.5, **Product Development and the Marketing Concept** (pages 191–198), in your textbook and use the following outline to make notes about the section.

Analytical Tools Surrounding Product Development

1. P_____ M_____

   _____
   _____
   _____
   _____
   _____
   _____

2. M_____ O_____ A_____

Part One	Part Two	Part Three

3. B_____ A_____

   _____
   _____
   _____
   _____
   _____
   _____

M. Analyzing Real-Life Business Situations: Product Development and the Marketing Concept

Product Mapping

Reread the case study on Sara Blakely on page 90. From the beginning, she had some significant obstacles to overcome. Now, new challenges are arising as larger companies begin to compete directly with her product. In the space below, create three product maps, each measuring different product characteristics, to illustrate how Spanx has positioned itself in the market. You might also use these maps to illustrate how Blakely might be able to address her new challenges and continue to differentiate her product from the competition.

Criteria used for each map:

1. _____

2. _____

3. _____

Marketing Opportunity Analysis

Complete a brief MOA for Spanx, based on the information provided in the case.

	Comments *(may include strengths and weaknesses, pricing, any other considerations affecting Spanx)*
overall market category: _____ _____	
indirect competitors: _____ _____	
direct competition: _____ _____	

Benefit Analysis

Do a benefit analysis for Spanx's product(s). What are the feature benefits for this product?

Feature	**Benefit**

Response to Threats

Explain two things that Blakely has done in response to the threats to her company.

1. _____

   _____

2. _____

   _____

N. Reviewing the Chapter

Multiple Choice

Circle the best response.

1. A feasibility study is designed to determine
   a) if any business opportunity is possible, practical, and viable
   b) how the marketing and production departments can work more efficiently together
   c) the best methods for cost cutting
   d) none of the above
   e) both a) and c) above

2. Idea screening is important because companies
   a) need to test consumer reactions
   b) need to analyze the competition
   c) need to develop a prototype
   d) none of the above
   e) both a) and b) above

3. Test marketing
   a) guarantees a new product's success
   b) tests consumer acceptance of the product
   c) is only done for high value products like cars
   d) none of the above
   e) both b) and c) above

4. An example of time utility include
   a) being able to purchase a bathing suit in the winter
   b) the convenience store that provides service 24 hours a day
   c) Butterball's information Web site because it is accessible 24 hours a day
   d) all of the above
   e) both a) and b) above

5. MOA consists of
   a) a situational analysis of the overall market, and indirect and direct competition
   b) an extensive research on trends and fads in a particular industry
   c) a review of marketing opportunities available to diversify a company's product line
   d) none of the above
   e) both b) and c) above

True/False

Circle T if the statement is true, F if it is false.

According to a marketing study in the *Journal of Product Innovation Management*, roughly 10 of 11 ideas are not commercially successful.   T   F

Basketball, the batteryless radio, and IMAX technology are all Canadian innovations.   T   F

When the computer market was less competitive, IBM is reported to have said, "The customer can have any colour they want as long as it is beige."   T   F

After an investment of hundreds of millions of dollars and 13 years of development, Gillette's Mach3 was finally introduced in 1990.   T   F

Word Scramble

Unscramble the following words.

PEPYTROOT

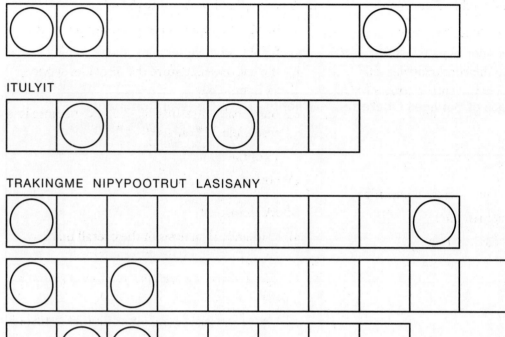

ITULYIT

TRAKINGME NIPYPOOTRUT LASISANY

PDTUCOR CALHUN

Using the circled letters, solve the riddle below.
Product managers do this to help find a way around the competition. (Hint: Think "Geography" class.)

___ ___ ___ ___ ___   ___ ___ ___ ___ ___ ___ ___ ___

Short Answer

1. Explain what is involved with the process of product mapping.

   _____

   _____

   _____

2. Explain the difference between a feature-benefit analysis and a cost-benefit analysis.

   _____

   _____

   _____

O. Marketing Plan: Product Development

Read page 202 in your textbook, **Marketing Plan**. Then complete these activities to help you with your marketing plan.

1. It is difficult for most entrepreneurs and small businesses to complete all the stages of the product development process. As a result, various companies throughout Canada and the United States provide this expertise. Conduct an Internet search and identify three companies that you would consider using to assist you in developing your product, service, or idea. Record your findings in the chart below.

Company Name/ Web Address	Types of Services Offered	Clients	General Comments (e.g., strengths, weaknesses, Web site)

Which company would you select to assist you? _____

Why? _____

_____

_____

2. Consider whether your product, service, or idea is an invention or an innovation.

Invention _____ Innovation _____ Explain your choice below.

_____

_____

If you are working with an invention, should you consider a patent? _____

3. In the middle column of the chart below, rate (1 for least important, 5 for very important) how important each stage of the product development process will be to the success of your product or service. In the right-hand column, list the tasks that will need to be accomplished at each stage, and who will be responsible for accomplishing these tasks.

Stage	Importance to Your Success (1–5)	What task will be required at each stage, and who will be responsible for doing it?
idea generation		
idea screening		
concept development		
market strategy		
feasibility study		
product design		
test marketing		
market entry		

4. Your product or service should have some unique selling points that distinguish it from the competition. Record these in the following chart to assist you in preparing the benefit analysis for your product or service. (Note: You may not necessarily have a feature for each element of "form utility.")

Type of Utility	Feature Analysis	Benefit Analysis
form		
place		
information		
time		
possession		

Chapter 6: Positioning and Branding

A. Understanding Key Terms: Chapter Introduction

Before reading this chapter, write what you think each term means in the middle column of this chart. After reading this chapter, complete the column on the right. How do your definitions and the textbook's compare?

Term	What Do You Think It Means?	Definition from Text
positioning		
target positioning		
product differentiation		
brand		
brand name		
private label		
logo		
slogan		
brand extension		
brand equity		
co-branding		
brand licensing		
proprietary design		

B. Understanding the Ideas: 6.1 What Is Positioning?

Read Section 6.1, **What is Positioning?** (pages 205–206), in your textbook and use the following to help guide your notetaking.

A position is _____

Positioning allows all of us to _____

_____

_____

_____

Marketers often take a position on their product or service. Explain. _____

_____

_____

_____

Top-of-the-mind awareness is sometimes referred to as _____

Many marketers define positioning as _____

_____

_____

_____

_____

_____

_____

_____

_____

_____

_____

What have you learned in this section? _____

_____

_____

_____

_____

_____

_____

_____

_____

_____

_____

C. Comparing Strategies: Positioning

1. Traditionally, Walt Disney World has marketed itself as a family vacation destination. One of its more recent advertisements, however, features a middle-aged man complaining to his mother that she and his father are going to Walt Disney World and not taking him with them. What is this saying about Disney's current positioning strategy?

_____

_____

_____

2. In 2002, Pepsi produced several high-energy (and high-priced) commercials featuring personalities such as Britney Spears and Mike Myers as Austin Powers. What does this say about Pepsi's positioning strategy? Do you think that you will see these same people on a Nescafe commercial? Why or why not?

_____

_____

_____

3. While Pepsi and Coca-Cola spend millions of dollars on advertising, there are lesser-known colas that do little to no advertising but still hold some market share. These brands usually position themselves as lower-priced alternatives. On the map below, position the following colas: Pepsi, Coca-Cola, Cott, RC, Buzz, No-name, President's Choice, a specialty "gourmet" cola that is brewed at a small café ($2.95 a bottle!), and a cola that your neighbour brews in his garage (20¢ to anyone brave enough to try it).

Well-Known Brand/Assumed Quality

Lower Price ⎯⎯⎯⎯⎯⎯⎯⎯⎯⎯⎯⎯⎯⎯⎯⎯⎯⎯ Higher Price

Unknown Brand/Unknown Quality

D. Understanding the Ideas: 6.2 Types of Positioning

As you read Section 6.2, **Types of Positioning** (pages 206–210), in your textbook, list and explain the five types of positioning. Provide an example for each from the textbook.

1. _____
_____
_____
_____

2. _____
_____
_____
_____

3. _____
_____
_____
_____

4. _____
_____
_____
_____

5. _____
_____
_____
_____

Identify at least three new pieces of information that you have learned in this section.

_____
_____
_____
_____
_____
_____

E. Assessing Slogans: Types of Positioning

1. Below is a list of five slogans. Indicate which type of positioning relates to each slogan.

   "Nothing comes between me and my Calvins" (Calvin Klein jeans) _____

   "Plop, plop, fizz, fizz—oh what a relief it is!" (Bayer's Alka-Seltzer®)_____

   "Billions and billions served" (McDonald's) _____

   "When it absolutely, positively has to be there overnight" (Federal Express) _____

   "Always Low Prices, Always Wal-Mart" (Wal-Mart) _____

2. Motivated by the need to expand its market and to respond to its critics, McDonald's has repositioned itself several times over the years. Explain how it has positioned itself in the following advertisements and state the type of positioning being used.

   a) Advertisements in the late 1960s and early 1970s had the slogan "Get a hamburger, fries, and drink and still get change back from a dollar."

   _____

   _____

   _____

   b) In about 1974, McDonald's advertisements began featuring the antics of cartoon-like characters such as Grimace, The Hamburglar, The Fry Guys, and Birdie (and Ronald McDonald, of course, who had been introduced in 1963).

   _____

   _____

   _____

   c) In the early 1980s, advertisements focused on fast breakfast foods featuring scenarios such as people in business attire car-pooling to work.

   _____

   _____

   _____

   d) Analyze current advertisements and explain how McDonald's seems to be, once again, repositioning itself.

   _____

   _____

   _____

F. Understanding the Ideas: 6.3 How to Position a Product

As you read Section 6.3, **How to Position a Product** (pages 212–215), in your textbook, complete the following questions.

The "positioning premise" is _____

_____

_____

The textbook presents some strategies for successfully positioning a product. Fill in the following chart.

Strategies for Successful Positioning	Example from Textbook

What have you learned in this section? _____

_____

_____

_____

In the following chart, provide an example of a company that has implemented the positioning strategy in the first column and explain how this strategy has been carried out. An example has been provided for you.

Positioning Strategy	Company	How the Strategy Is Carried Out
clear and coherent	Tim Hortons	In-store displays, cups, signs, advertising all state that Tim Hortons' products are always fresh.
long-term positioning		
relevant positioning		
clear and coherent positioning		
distinctive positioning		

H. Understanding the Ideas: 6.4 Branding

As you read Section 6.4, **Branding** (pages 216–221), in your textbook, describe and/or respond to the following:

Product differentiation is _____

_____

_____

_____

A brand is_____

_____

_____

_____

Two types of brand names are:

1. _____

    Examples _____

2. _____

    Examples _____

A logo is_____

There are three forms of logos:

1. _____

2. _____

3. _____

A slogan is _____

Characteristics of a good slogan are _____

_____

_____

_____

_____

_____

_____

I. Identifying Real-Life Examples: Branding

1. Identify the name of the company that is associated with each of the following logos:

 _____

 _____

 _____

2. Match each slogan to the appropriate organization listed below.

____ Just Do It

____ Membership has its privileges

____ Always

____ Why buy a mattress anywhere else?

____ A Different Kind of Company, a Different Kind of Car

1. Rebok   6. Nike

2. Sleep Country Canada   7. City Mattresses

3. Ford   8. Saturn

4. VISA   9. American Express

5. Coca-Cola   10. Pepsi

J. Writing a Rationale: Branding

Create a logo and slogan for two of the following businesses and, based on what you have read in your textbook, explain why you think these would be effective.

Jack's Burger Shack, Gina's Hair Salon, Joe's Paving Company, Royal Courier Inc.

1. _____

Slogan: _____

_____

_____

_____

_____

_____

_____

Rationale: _____

_____

_____

_____

_____

2. _____

Slogan: _____

_____

_____

_____

_____

_____

_____

Rationale: _____

_____

_____

_____

_____

As you read Section 6.5, **Brand Strategies** (pages 221–226), in your textbook, complete the following notetaking organizer.

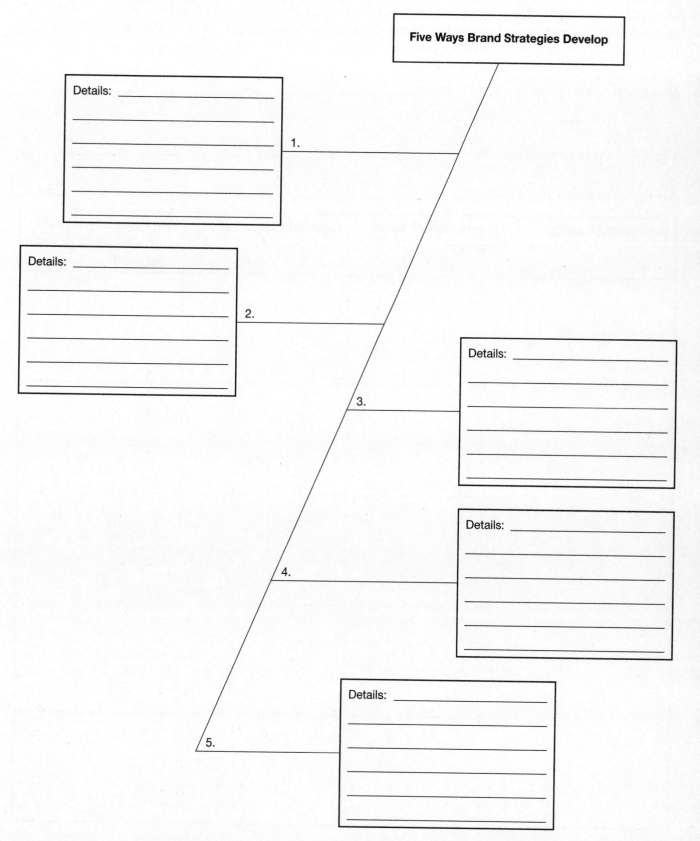

Five Ways Brand Strategies Develop

Details: _____

_____

_____

_____

_____

1.

2.

Details: _____

_____

_____

_____

_____

3. Details: _____

_____

_____

_____

_____

_____

4. Details: _____

_____

_____

_____

_____

_____

5. Details: _____

_____

_____

_____

_____

Imagine that you are the owner of a small- to medium-sized company. (You can decide what kind of business you are in.) You currently produce only one or two primary products, though you may also produce some secondary products that make up a small part of your business. You have been successful with your primary products, but you only service a fairly small segment of the market. Describe how you will use the five brand strategies to grow your business in the coming years.

Describe your small/medium-sized business. _____

_____

What is/are your primary brand(s)? _____

Are there any secondary brands? _____

Branding Strategy	Description of Your Strategy	Desired Outcome	Are there any threats to the success of your strategy?

M. Charting Real-World Examples: Co-Branding Strategies

Co-branding can be a very effective branding strategy. Companies that market food products tend to participate in co-branding. Visit a local grocery store and identify five examples of co-branding. Complete the following chart.

Co-Branding Example (e.g., Crest and Scope)	How the Companies Co-Branded (e.g., a new product, advertising, promotional tie-ins)	Which company do you think will benefit more from the partnership? (e.g. financially, brand equity)

As you read Section 6.6, **Branding for International Markets** (page 227–230), in your textbook, complete the chart below, filling in the details for each consideration when deciding on an international branding strategy.

International business is increasing because _____

_____

centralized or decentralized organization

Details: _____

_____

_____

Details: _____

_____

_____

Details: _____

_____

_____

Details: _____

_____

_____

Details: _____

_____

_____

Details: _____

_____

_____

Details: _____

_____

_____

Details: _____

_____

_____

Read this case study and answer the questions that follow.

Pampers Took Rebranding to Heart

By Danny Kucharsky

MONTREAL: Removing the image of a Caucasian baby and replacing it with a heart symbol was the key to revitalizing the Pampers brand worldwide.

The stylized heart—which symbolizes the mother/baby relationship—was an integral part of repositioning the Procter & Gamble brand in the late 1990s as a total baby care business, delegates to the 13th International Corporate/Brand Identity Conference of the Boston-based Design Management Institute were told in Montreal earlier this month.

The repositioning also allowed the company to extend the Pampers brand into such products as baby apparel and Bibsters, a line of disposable bibs that P&G launched in the United States, according to Cincinnati-based Tom Dierking, global associate design director for P&G, and Jerome Kathman, president and CEO of the international design firm and P&G client Libby Perszyk Kathman.

Launched in 1961, the multi-billion dollar Pampers brand had different looks worldwide by the 1990s, as design decisions were often made by local management. "We weren't managing three-to-five-year planning," Dierking says. The new global design for the brand was implemented by 1997, but that wasn't enough, Kathman adds.

P&G staffers went world-wide interviewing consumers, visiting pharmacies and small retailers, and came to the realization the baby image "was not an equity," and was not contributing to the brand's success, Kathman says.

The baby image was replaced by the heart as part of a mission to think baby care, not diapers, he says, and to think brand identity, not packaging. The new brand image expresses joy and warmth and great empathy, and fits an era in which major corporations are trying to act more folksy, Kathman explains.

"The newly empowered consumer expects more from brands," says Dierking, adding P&G is developing one-on-one relationships with parents via its Web site, pampers.com.

Source: Marketing Magazine, June 25, 2001. Contents copyright 1996 – 2001 by Rogers Media Inc. All rights reserved.

1. Why did Pampers change its branding stregy? _____

   _____

   _____

   _____

   _____

   _____

   _____

2. What was Procter & Gamble hoping to achieve by changing Pamper's logo? _____

   _____

   _____

   _____

   _____

   _____

   _____

   _____

   _____

   _____

3. Imagine that Pampers has the ability to customize its logo for every country. Rather than using the heart symbol, it keeps the baby as part of its logo but changes the baby's image to reflect the dominant culture of the country in which the product is being sold. Do you think this alternative approach would be effective? Would it achieve all the objectives that the heart symbol set out to achieve? Explain.

   _____

   _____

   _____

   _____

   _____

   _____

   _____

   _____

   _____

   _____

   _____

   _____

As you read Section 6.7, **Packaging** (pages 232–238), in your textbook, complete the following concept map.

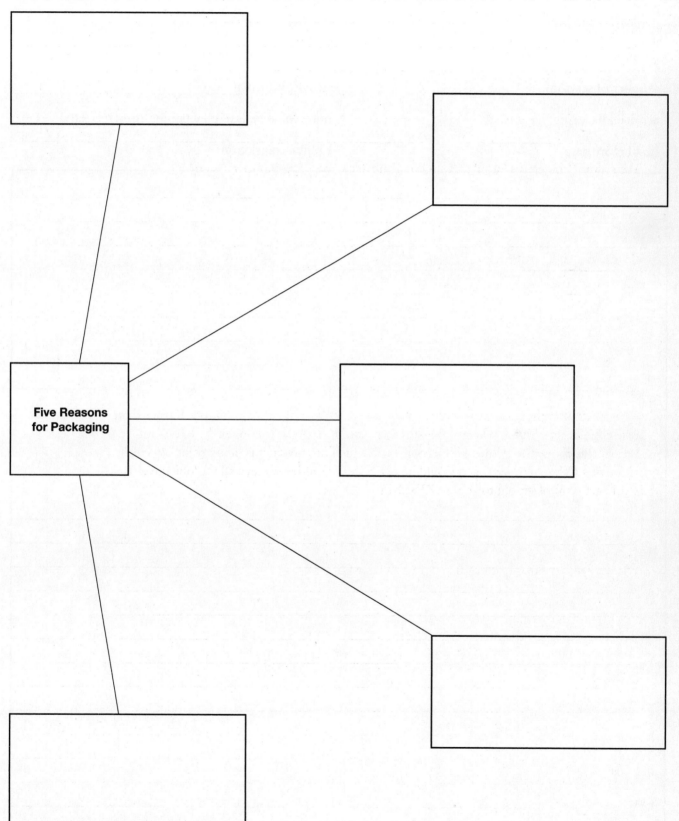

Five Reasons for Packaging

Create a label for a food product of your choice. Use the space provided below to illustrate what your label might look like. The following criteria must be met for label design:

- name of the brand

- name and address of the manufacturer

- number of servings

- artificial flavoring

- best before date

- net quantity of the product

- ingredients (heaviest listed first)

- storage information

- nutritional facts (e.g., vitamins, minerals, etc.)

- French translations

Multiple Choice

Circle the best response.

1. To gain an effective target market position, all of a brand's marketing must be focused on
   a) many consumer segments
   b) a specific consumer segment
   c) more than one consumer segment
   d) international markets

2. There are _____ types of positioning that a business might use.
   a) two
   b) three
   c) four
   d) five

3. In terms of the reasons for packaging, consolidation means
   a) eliminating or minimizing waste
   b) packaging similar products together
   c) to contain the product and keep it all together
   d) making a package smaller so it is easier to transport

True/False

Indicate whether the statement is true (T) or false (F).

_____ Price positioning could mean attempting to be the most expensive product in a category.

_____ A brand is the visual image that marketers create to allow consumers to identify their particular product or service.

_____ A monogramatic logo is usually line drawings of people.

_____ A brand extension is when a company uses one of its established brands to create a similar product that capitalizes on the older brand's success.

_____ Co-branding is when two or more brands combine to co-operate for their mutual benefit.

_____ A decentralized organization would be more likely to maintain the same brand in all markets.

_____ Ingredients are required by law to be listed in ascending order.

_____ Proprietary design means that the shapes or colour of the package can only be used by the manufacturers of the product.

Short Answer

1. How can a business use price positioning to discourage customers that it doesn't want?

   _____

   _____

   _____

2. Explain the expansion strategy when branding for international markets.

   _____

   _____

   _____

3. How can some products have cultural associations that are negative?

   _____

   _____

   _____

4. List some of the materials used by manufacturers to package fragile products.

   _____

   _____

   _____

5. Why must packaging be environmentally friendly in today's environment?

   _____

   _____

   _____

Cryptogram

Solve the following cryptogram and discover the hidden marketing message. Clues to get you started: Each "U" in the puzzle is a "G," each "N" is a "B," each "A" is an "N," and each "V" is a "P."

N B R A J Q A U   M F B   R   M F B T Q U A

W R B S T C   J T V T A J Z   F A   " U Y F N R Y

V F Z Q C Q F A Q A U . "

S. Marketing Plan: Positioning and Branding

Work through the following to build on the marketing plan you started in Chapter 1.

Differentiating your product from the competition is the most effective way to attract your target market! You differentiate your product from the competition by choosing a unique name, logo, slogan(s), and packaging for your product.

Positioning Strategy—*What will be your positioning strategy and why? (e.g., benefit, target, price, distribution, and service)*	Positioning Factors—*How do you plan to account for the following positioning factors?*	Name of Brand—*Will your name be corporate dominant or product dominant? Explain in detail.*
	positioning premise:	
	long-term positioning:	
	relevant positioning:	
	clear and coherent positioning:	
	distinctive positioning:	

Logo and Slogan(s)

Will your logo be monogramatic, a visual symbol, or an abstract symbol? Illustrate below how your logo will look. Keep in mind the characteristics of a "good" logo as outlined on pages 218–220 in your textbook. You may want to also visit the Internet to get further information on logo design.

What will your slogan(s) be? Write down at least five slogans that can be associated with each of the positioning factors outlined above.

_____
_____
_____
_____
_____
_____
_____

Packaging and Label Design

What materials will be used to make and to protect your package? Will they be environmentally friendly? How?

_____
_____
_____
_____
_____
_____
_____

Create Your Packaging

Illustrate below how your package will look. Keep in mind the shape and colour of your package. Both elements must be in line with how you plan to position the product to your target market. Include all of the information that will be on your package. Read pages 232–235 in your textbook to ensure that you have included all the information that is required by Canadian law.

CHAPTER 7: Pricing

A. Understanding Key Terms: Chapter Introduction

Before reading this chapter, write what you think each term means in the middle column of this chart. After reading this chapter, complete the column on the right. How do your definitions and the textbook's compare?

Term	What Do You Think It Means?	Definition from Text
markup		
margin		
variable costs		
fixed costs		
break-even point		
economy of scale		
price-fixing		
msrp		
bait and switch		
skimming		
marketing boards		
price lining		

Read Section 7.1, **Determining the Price** (pages 245–253), in your textbook, then fill in the missing information.

The two main factors that determine price are:

1. _____

2. _____

Five other pricing considerations are 1) _____, 2) _____,

3) _____, 4) _____, 5) _____.

A break-even analysis is_____ _____ _____		
Variable costs are	Fixed costs are	
Gross profit or _____ = _____ - _____		

_____ (BEP) = _____ ÷ _____

Economies of scale are _____

_____

_____

Four ways that marketers use economies of scale are:

1. _____

2. _____

3. _____

4. _____

Diseconomies of scale happen when a company becomes too large. This results in_____

_____

_____

_____

C. Calculating Profit: Gross Profit and Break-Even Point

1. Fill in the missing information in the following chart. (Hint: In this scenario, neither total fixed cost nor variable cost per unit changes, regardless of the quantities you produce.)

	1	50	100	500	1000	2000	10 000
total fixed cost	$18 000						
total variable cost							
total cost							
fixed cost per unit							
variable cost per unit	$22						
total cost per unit							

2. Your company has decided to charge $50 for the product in the above scenario.

   a) Calculate the break-even point.

   b) Suppose your company demands a margin of 15% on any product it decides to produce. What effect does this have on your break-even point? [Remember: Margin % = (selling price per unit ÷ total cost per unit) × 100]

3. Consider the following two scenarios and explain the possible effects on the pricing margins and profits for the product. If possible, suggest what the company could do in response to these conditions.

   a) Your company is doing very well. The production for its own sales, combined with the product it manufactures for private brands, totals 10 000 units. To meet this demand, it has merged with a smaller company to take advantage of its machines and floor space. As a result, there is internal strife. Expensive layoffs are needed, higher salaries are required for people who know how to operate the new machinery, and overlapping resources are causing inefficiencies in the operations.

   _____

   _____

   _____

   _____

   _____

   _____

   _____

   _____

   _____

   _____

   _____

   b) The success of your company in the marketplace has not gone unnoticed by competitors. Where there used to be only one competitor, two new companies are starting up and they have a tremendous amount of capital behind them. They have also hired away some of your expertise. As if this wasn't bad enough, there is talk of a very large US company making a move into the Canadian market.

   _____

   _____

   _____

   _____

   _____

   _____

   _____

   _____

   _____

   _____

   _____

   _____

D. Understanding the Ideas:
7.2 Additional Factors Affecting Price

Read Section 7.2, **Additional Factors Affecting Price** (pages 255–260), in your textbook, then fill in the missing information.

Laws

Three deceptive pricing practices are (include a description):

1. _____

2. _____

3. _____

The functions of marketing boards are _____

_____

_____

_____

Product Positioning

Two pricing strategies to position a product are (include a description):

1. _____

_____

2. _____

_____

Consumer Demand

Demand affects price because _____

_____

_____

_____

_____

Competition plays a role in demand because _____

_____

_____

_____

_____

Vitamin Price-Fixing

If you eat any food that is vitamin enriched, such as bread, milk, or cereal, you may have been paying more than you should have. That's because some of the world's biggest multinational corporations conspired to raise the price of vitamins and vitamin additives. It was the largest price fixing scam in the world. Now a Canadian consumers' group is fighting for compensation.

The price-fixing in the vitamin industry went on for more than ten years as some of the world's most powerful companies secretly orchestrated the conspiracy. They jacked up the price of vitamins in hundreds of products.

Five of the world's leading vitamin producers have pleaded guilty to price-fixing. Smaller players have also admitted their role. Now, Canada's largest consumer group wants compensation.

André-Bernard Guévin has taken his concerns to Option consommateurs, a Quebec consumer group. The group argues that Canadians deserve a chunk of the price-fixers' profits.

"To compensate consumers who had to pay more," Jannick Desforges of Option consommateurs told Marketplace of the reason for the lawsuit. "Because the consumers at the end were the victims of this big conspiracy."

The organization has hired Montreal class-action lawyer Eric David to pursue the case. He says the price-fixing documents filed with the federal Competition Bureau read like a spy thriller.

"The illegal profits that these companies made came out of the pockets of consumers," David told Marketplace. "Every single consumer in Canada. And they have to be compensated, because a wrong was committed."

Secret meetings to plot strategy

Members of the vitamin cartel pleaded guilty in 1999.

Here's how their scheme worked: companies like Hoffman LaRoche of Switzerland, Rhone Poulenc of France, BASF of Germany, and two Japanese companies—Eisai Company Limited and Daiichi Pharmaceutical—secretly met in hotels and homes around the world. Instead of competing for business, they agreed on how much of each product they would sell and how much they would charge for it.

An FBI investigation resulted in rare behind the scenes video.

The video shows executives from multinational firms agreeing to fix global prices for an additive in animal feed.

A tiny camera hidden in a lamp recorded meetings of corporate executives, carving up world markets. The group claimed it was holding trade association talks was in fact staging secret conspiracy meetings.

The video caught the so-called competitors wining and dining each other, calling each other "friend" and labelling the consumer as the enemy....

Over the years, the vitamin companies saw sales of more than $700 million in Canada. Option consommateur figures every Canadian man, woman, and child is owed $5....

Cartel impoverished everyone: economist

Price fixing schemes like this one often don't get heavy media coverage because they are white collar crimes, according to Richard Schwindt, an economist at Simon Fraser University near Vancouver.

"If you had a bank robbery, or an embezzlement that involved those sums of monies," Schwindt told Marketplace, "it would be front page news.

"It's not like we're fixing the prices of mink coats. We're fixing the prices of basic commodities, which means all consumers are slightly impoverished by this type of behaviour. And generally, it's a reallocation from those that have less to those that have more."...

Economist Richard Schwindt suggests that consumers are likely duped by cartels more often than we think.

"How do you know, each time you go into the marketplace and you buy something, that it isn't ten percent more than it would be absent an agreement between competitors?" Schwindt asks. "There's no way in the world that you could detect this."

To fight such cartels, the Competition Bureau has created an immunity program. The first company involved in a cartel that comes forward and confesses about a price-fixing scheme is protected from prosecution. The goal is to create cartel uncertainty.

"Imagine a meeting where one of your competitors all of a sudden doesn't appear," the bureau's Jean-Claude Drapeau says. "You may think that he's talking to us, which is what we want to create."

The immunity program appears to be working. The Competition Bureau says its investigators are working full-time on a number of cartel investigations—and new price-fixing leads come in every month.

Source: Excerpted from
http://cbc.ca/consumers/market/files/health/vitamins/index.html
(CBC Marketplace)

1. Briefly describe the price-fixing scandal.

_____

_____

_____

2. Why, according to the various quoted sources, is price-fixing wrong and punishable by law?

_____

_____

_____

3. If price-fixing is illegal, why do you think it still occurs?

_____

_____

_____

4. What measure has now been put in place to prevent cartels from duping consumers? How does it work?

_____

_____

_____

5. Using print and/or Internet sources, research other cases of illegal pricing practices. Briefly describe each situation. What were the penalties?

_____

_____

_____

F. Listing Examples: Price Sensitivity

Make a list of five products that are price sensitive and five products that are price insensitive.

Price Sensitive	Price Insensitive
1.	1.
2.	2.
3.	3.
4.	4.
5.	5.

G. Understanding the Ideas: 7.3 Pricing Strategies

Complete the following chart as you read Section 7.3, **Pricing Strategies** (pages 260–265), in your textbook.

Strategy	Definition	Examples
market skimming		
penetration pricing		
competitive pricing		
benchmark pricing (follow the leader pricing)		

What have you learned in this section? _____

_____

_____

_____

_____

H. Making Connections: Cartels and the Price of Gasoline

In your textbook, you read about the OPEC cartel and its attempt to control market conditions in the North American oil markets. There were dramatic social and economic consequences because of its efforts.

1. What is a cartel? _____
   _____
   _____
   _____

2. OPEC is still in existence and yet it does not have the same global influence. Why not? Use the Internet and/or other print sources to find out why. _____
   _____
   _____
   _____

3. What other factors affect the price of gasoline in your community? _____
   _____
   _____
   _____

4. Some service stations and integrated oil companies are sensitive about the price of gasoline. Visit three stations, owned by different companies, in person or on the Internet and record how these companies explain the cost of a litre of gasoline.

Company	Explanation

As you read Section 7.4, **Pricing Policies** (pages 267–273), in your textbook, fill in the information about how businesses set pricing policies.

Leader pricing is _____
_____
_____
_____
_____

Price lining is _____
_____
_____
_____
_____
_____

Everyday low prices is _____
_____
_____
_____
_____

Super sizing is _____
_____
_____
_____
_____
_____

Negotiated pricing is _____
_____
_____
_____
_____

Interest-free pricing is _____
_____
_____
_____
_____
_____

Combo pricing is _____
_____
_____
_____
_____

Psychological pricing is _____
_____
_____
_____
_____

Return on investment (ROI) is _____
_____
_____
_____
_____

Purchase discounts are _____
_____
_____
_____
_____

J. Matching the Concepts: Pricing Policies

Match each of the following scenarios on the left with the most correct pricing policy on the right.

_____ Alyson's grocery store guarantees its customers the lowest price in town on milk and bread.

_____ An electronics shop advertises a digital camera at cost (i.e., without any markup) to bring people into the store.

_____ In a recent slump in sales, many car dealers offered to sell their cars with 0% financing.

_____ The pricing policy that has retailers price their products at $11.95 rather than $12.

_____ This is why a large store can sell the same product cheaper than small stores.

_____ A situation where a buyer refuses to pay the advertised price, so the buyer and seller decide on a lower price.

_____ A manufacturer has one price for golf shirts at Stelle's Discount World and another for the golf shirts sold at the pro shop of the private country club.

A. everyday low prices

B. interest-free pricing

C. leader pricing

D. super sizing

E. price lining

F. psychological pricing

G. negotiated pricing

H. volume discount

I. early payment discount

Complete the following chart.

List Price	Volume Discount Rate	Volume Discount	Net Price
$600	22%		
$1725	36.5%		
$900	35%		
	40%	$160	$240

Complete the following chart.

Date of Invoice	Date Goods Received	Terms	Last Day of Discount Period	End of Credit Period
June 18		2/10, n/30		
February 3		1/30, n/60		
August 5	October 7	2/10, n/30 ROG		

L. Understanding the Ideas:
7.5 Pricing for the International Market

Read Section 7.5, **Pricing for the International Market** (pages 274–280), in your textbook and fill in the following information.

The four factors affecting international pricing are:

1. _____

2. _____

3. _____

4. _____

Tariffs are_____

_____

_____

_____

_____

Three types of tariff rates are:

1. _____

2. _____

3. _____

Transportation costs are a concern because _____

_____

_____

_____

_____

Containerization can alleviate transportation costs by _____

_____

_____

_____

_____

Examples of extra charges are _____

_____

_____

_____

M. Researching on the Internet: Currency Values

1. Some of Canada's major trading partners are listed in this table. Complete the chart using current foreign exchange rates. These can be found in some daily newspapers or on the Internet. The Bank of Canada Web site (www.bankofcanada.ca) has a currency converter.

Country	Currency	Value of 1 Currency Unit in Canadian Dollars	Value of $1 CDN in the Country's Currency
United States			
Mexico			
Japan			
China			
United Kingdom			
European Union			

2. Some travellers don't compare currency exchange rates. Instead, they change their money at the most convenient outlet they can find. Rates from banks or foreign exchange brokers are usually better than those offered by some hotels, stores, and airport exchange booths. Develop your own survey of exchange rates for American dollars offered in your community. What do banks, stores, hotels, or other outlets offer as an exchange rate? Record your research in this chart.

Location	Exchange Rate Offered	Official Rate	% Difference

N. Extending Knowledge: Pricing for the International Market

1. People travelling are often surprised to find that some items are priced much higher or much lower abroad than in their country. From your own experience or that of friends or family, or by researching on the Internet, find four examples of products that cost much more or much less abroad than they cost at home.

Product	Cost at Home	Cost Abroad

2. For the following major trading partners, find out what Canada's tariff relationship is with them. Your textbook and the Department of Foreign Affairs and International Trade Web site (www.dfait-maeci.gc.ca) are good places to start.

Country	Tariff Designation	Special Treaties?
United States		
Japan		
China		
United Kingdom		
Mexico		
Taiwan		

O. Assessing Real-Life Situations: Pricing for the International Market

1. Purchasing power parity is a term used to describe why, over time, the dollar price of a good in one country should equal its dollar price in all other countries. While this theory relies on many assumptions, it is naturally appealing. The notion that a DVD should sell for the same dollar price in Canada as it does in the United States or the United Kingdom makes sense in terms of supply and demand in world markets. Suppose that the DVD sells for $19.95 in Canada, $14.95 in the United States, and £49.90 in the United Kingdom.

   In which country is the dollar price of the DVD the lowest? In which is it the highest? The answer to this depends on current foreign exchange rates.

   _____

   _____

   _____

2. McDonald's restaurants operate in 116 countries around the world. Most sell McDonald's trademark "Big Mac." Because the Big Mac is made the same way with the same ingredients everywhere, its price in each country can be measured against other currencies to determine whether a particular currency is over- or under-valued. If a Big Mac in Newark, Delaware, costs $1.79 (US) and that same Big Mac made in Blind River, Ontario, costs $2.99 (Cdn), then technically, the only difference between the two prices should be the level of the Canada–US currency exchange rate. The same theory applies to every country in the world where McDonald's sells the Big Mac. In practice, the prices are not the same. If they were, then the Big Mac in Canada would cost, before taxes, $2.80 based on a $0.64 exchange rate.

   Every April, _The Economist_ magazine publishes "The Big Mac Index" to determine what currencies should be worth based on the cost of the sandwich. It's not a perfect measurement. Prices are distorted by trade barriers on beef, sales taxes, and other non-food cost differences. Most emerging market currencies are undervalued against the US dollar based on Big Mac analysis.

   Obtain a copy of the most recent Big Mac Index from _The Economist_ or visit its Web site (www.economist.com).

   a) From the Big Mac Index, which countries have the most overvalued currencies? Offer an explanation for why this might be true.

   _____

   _____

   _____

   b) How does Canada compare with its largest trading partners (the United States, Mexico, China, and Japan in particular)? Is the Canadian dollar overvalued or undervalued based on Big Macs?

   _____

   _____

   _____

Word Search

Find the words listed below in the following puzzle.

```
E  B  A  I  T  A  N  D  S  W  I  T  C  H  I  S  X  N  T  C
L  E  X  B  T  N  O  T  E  Q  B  Y  O  S  J  N  I  O  I  O
A  N  B  S  R  T  I  F  O  R  P  S  S  O  R  G  Q  B  F  S
C  C  G  E  P  E  N  A  B  S  F  L  F  M  R  Z  F  D  O  T
S  H  N  M  Y  O  A  C  E  K  J  P  I  A  B  I  R  Q  R  B
F  M  I  C  A  D  C  K  P  I  A  W  M  Q  X  A  S  V  P  A
O  A  X  N  S  R  Q  D  E  M  A  N  D  E  O  V  L  I  Y  S
Y  R  I  Y  G  R  K  S  P  V  O  Y  D  B  X  I  Z  G  V  E
M  K  F  F  M  J  C  E  A  I  E  C  G  N  J  S  D  Z  U  D
O  P  E  N  E  T  R  A  T  I  O  N  P  R  I  C  I  N  G  P
N  R  C  F  N  Y  K  U  R  S  I  Y  A  P  U  K  R  A  M  R
O  I  I  P  L  A  B  C  T  T  K  N  C  N  N  B  Q  L  H  I
C  C  R  P  Y  I  T  S  E  T  E  I  G  M  A  I  Y  Y  Z  C
E  E  P  W  R  O  F  K  Z  O  W  L  M  L  D  L  G  U  Z  I
V  U  B  T  D  C  R  I  D  F  A  B  M  M  Y  A  Y  R  Y  N
S  P  N  R  R  A  P  R  I  C  E  L  I  N  I  N  G  S  A  G
Q  O  S  Y  M  H  W  A  E  I  U  K  V  F  S  N  G  T  I  M
C  P  R  E  M  I  U  M  P  R  I  C  I  N  G  I  G  A  R  S
S  T  S  O  C  E  L  B  A  I  R  A  V  R  H  K  X  A  L  J
G  N  I  T  E  K  C  I  T  E  L  B  U  O  D  U  D  S  V  Y
```

bait and switch

benchmark price

BEP

break-even analysis

cartel

contribution margin

cost based pricing

demand

double ticketing

economy of scale

fixed costs

gross profit

margin

marketing board

market skimming

markup

penetration pricing

premium pricing

price fixing

price lining

profit

supply

variable costs

Multiple Choice

Circle the best response.

1. A business intentionally priced its products extremely low in order to make them immediately appealing to the mass market. This strategy is known as
   a) skimming
   b) penetration
   c) prestige
   d) odd pricing

2. A strategy of setting an initially high price for a product or service before competitors enter into the market is called
   a) skimming
   b) penetration
   c) odd pricing
   d) loss leader pricing

3. Businesses that conspire to set prices for a specific product are involved in
   a) retail price maintenance
   b) price-fixing
   c) double ticketing
   d) bait and switch pricing

4. What is the break-even point in units for a product with a selling price of $28, related fixed costs of $178 878, and per unit costs of $21?
   a) 3651 units
   b) 6389 units
   c) 8158 units
   d) 25 554 units

True/False

Circle T if the statement is true, F if it is false.

1. Variable costs are directly dependent upon how many goods are sold.   T   F

2. Gross profit is the selling price plus the variable cost.   T   F

3. Return on investments is the overall revenue and profit of yearly sales.   T   F

Fill in the Blanks

1. A _____ is a reduction in unit cost for a large order quantity.

2. _____ is a conspiracy among businesses to set prices for a product.

Q. Marketing Plan: Pricing

1. You have already identified a product or service for your marketing plan in the previous chapters. If it is a new product or service, set an introductory price. Use these questions to guide you.

At what price will the product or service be introduced?	
What pricing strategy are you using to set that price? Explain.	
What objectives will be accomplished by using this strategy? Explain.	
Why is the product worth its price?	
Do you foresee being able to take advantage of economies of scale either now or in the future?	
What prices do the major competitors charge?	
How price sensitive is the product or service?	
How will the final price contribute to the product or service's position?	
Are there any pricing policies that should be used to calculate the price?	
How do you foresee the price changing as your product or service goes through the product life cycle?	

2. Do a **SWOT** analysis on your pricing strategy. What are the **S**trengths, **W**eaknesses, **O**pportunities, and **T**hreats that your pricing strategy raises?

a) Strengths: _____

_____

_____

_____

_____

_____

_____

b) Weaknesses: _____

_____

_____

_____

_____

_____

_____

c) Opportunities: _____

_____

_____

_____

_____

_____

_____

d) Threats: _____

_____

_____

_____

_____

_____

_____

_____

CHAPTER 8: Distribution and Logistics

A. Understanding Key Terms: Chapter Introduction

Before reading this chapter, write what you think each term means in the middle column of this chart. After reading this chapter, complete the column on the right. How do your definitions and the textbook's compare?

Term	What Do You Think It Means?	Definition from Text
channels of distribution		
logistics		
intermediaries		
intensive distribution		
selective distribution		
direct channel		
importers		
wholesalers		
retailing		
specialty channels		
channel captains		
Free on Board (F.O.B.)		

B. Understanding the Ideas: 8.1 Channels of Distribution

Read Section 8.1, **Channels of Distribution** (pages 287–291), in your textbook and fill in the missing information in the following chart.

Distribution Policy	Description	Example from the Textbook

What have you learned in this section? _____

_____

_____

_____

_____

_____

C. Researching the Internet: Channels of Distribution

Investigate the channels of distribution used by the following companies. To start, you could visit their Web sites: Froster (www.froster.ca), Nelson Thomson Learning (www.nelson.com), COWS (www.cows.ca), William Ashley (www.williamashley.com), Viceroy Homes Limited (www.viceroy.com), Reid's Dairy (www.reidsdairy.com), and Roots (www.roots.ca).

1. Do any of these companies use intensive distribution? Explain your answer.

_____

_____

_____

_____

_____

2. Do any of these businesses use selective distribution? Explain your answer.

_____

_____

_____

_____

_____

3. Do any of these businesses use exclusive distribution? Explain your answer.

_____

_____

_____

_____

_____

4. Do any of these businesses use integrated distribution? Explain your answer.

_____

_____

_____

_____

_____

5. How is the Internet changing the structure of distribution channels?

_____

_____

_____

_____

_____

Below is the start of a graphic organizer. As you read Section 8.2, **Types of Channels** (pages 293–306), in your textbook, map out the rest of the organizer, briefing describing each concept.

Direct Channels (description):

_____

_____

Indirect Channels (description):

_____

_____

Importers:	Wholesalers:	Retailers:

E. Charting Relationships: Indirect Channels

Although some manufacturers sell directly to consumers, most sell through importers, retailers, wholesalers, or other distributors because these intermediaries provide important services. The following graph shows how products are distributed using intermediaries.

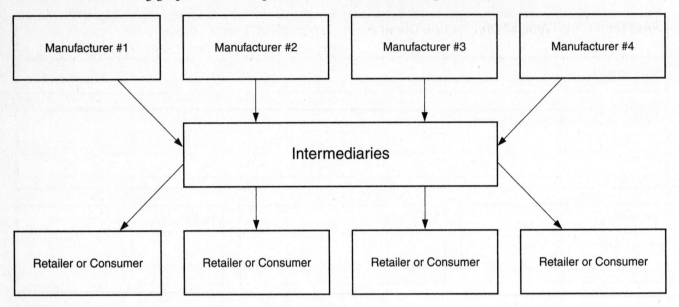

What would the above graphic look like without intermediaries? Each retailer or consumer would have to access the manufacturer directly and vice versa. Redraw the above graph to show what distribution might look like without intermediaries *and* the functions that they provide.

From your redrawn graph, what can you conclude about the importance of intermediaries to both manufacturers and retailers? _____

_____

_____

For each of the following products and services, suggest the best channel of distribution: direct, indirect (specify the intermediary type), specialty channel (specify the type), or a combination. Explain your choice of distribution channel(s).

Product	Type of Distribution Channel	Explanation *(consider the product or service, the advantages, the channel functions, etc.)*
toothpaste		
lumber		
veterinarian		
potato chips		
CD with classical music		
china		
duct cleaning		
golf shoes		
finely tailored clothing		

Read Section 8.3, **What to Consider When Selecting a Distribution Channel** (pages 308–312), in your textbook and complete the following map.

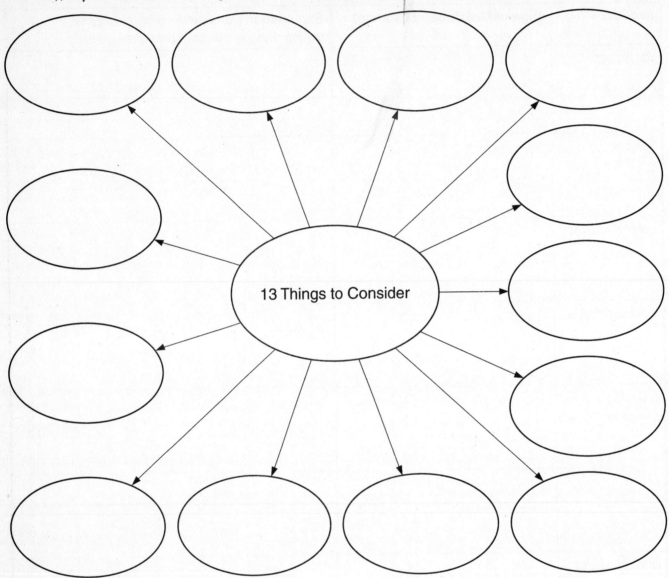

Fill in the following information.

Channel Captain	Description	Example from Textbook

H. Assessing Factors:
What to Consider When Selecting a Distribution Channel

The 13 considerations outlined in the textbook could be divided into four categories of factors: market, product, consumer, and channel factors. Choose one of the following products or services and list how these factors will affect your choice of distribution channel: bottled water, pizza, clothing for teenagers, snow shovel, talking book, steel, pet grooming, forklift, or banking (or a product or service of your own choosing).

Product: _____

Market Factors *(market size, market location, technology)*	**Product Factors** *(seasonal or high fashion, custom made, perishability, value, size and weight, warranty, price sensitivity)*
Consumer Factors *(type of consumer, income level, buying habits)*	**Channel Factors** *(competitive advantage)*

Read Section 8.4, **Logistics** (pages 312–318), in your textbook and fill in the missing information.

Logistics is _____

_____

Determining the appropriate transportation method for shipping product:

Major Factors	Considerations When Deciding Whether to Use
1.	
2.	
3.	
4.	

Transportation:

Transportation Method	Reasons Why It Is Used	Example of When It Is Used
1.		
2.		
3.		
4.		
5.		

J. Researching the Internet: Logistics

Logistics is not just storing and moving inventory, it is also knowing where the goods are throughout the supply chain, and finding alternative shipping modes and routes to quickly get around delayed and irregular shipments. The importance of these efforts is illustrated by the circumstances at General Motors Corp. and Ford Motor Co. after the terrorist attacks in New York on September 11, 2001. Automotive manufacturing came to a temporary halt at these companies' Ontario plants because just-in-time (JIT) deliveries were delayed at the Canadian–US border. Delays at the Mexican border also caused Ford to also shorten production for about two days at two of its Mexican assembly plants.

The goal of effective distribution logistics is to create a quick, smooth channel from material source (supplier) to material consumption (customer), while responding to the real-time problems that occur from changing customer requirements, routings, transportation modes, and international trade requirements. To achieve these objectives, numerous industry processes and practices have been developed, including quick response, continuous replenishment, efficient consumer response, and JIT and vendor-managed inventory.

It is without question that strong logistics is a competitive advantage. Because of this, companies invest both time and money into developing effective processes. AMR Research suggests that organizations spend 11% of their revenues on logistics. Interestingly enough, despite the recognized importance of these processes, they are some of the last core business processes to be automated! More often than not, logistics is an in-house, manual process involving homegrown inventory, warehouse, and transportation management systems.

1. a) Go to the Council of Logistic Management's Web site at www.clm1.org. Find two Canadian logistics organizations. Record their URLs here.

   _____

   _____

   b) Go to one of these Web sites and describe the type of services and information it offers.

   _____

   _____

   _____

2. Find out from various sources how the events of September 11, 2001, affected the Canadian automotive industry. What issues have arisen out of these events? How have events shaped future distribution practices? Visit the Automotive Parts Manufacturers' Association Web site (www.apma.ca) as a starting point for your research.

   _____

   _____

   _____

   _____

   _____

   _____

   _____

   _____

Read Section 8.5, **Inventory Management** (pages 318–323), in your textbook and fill in the information in the following notetaking diagram.

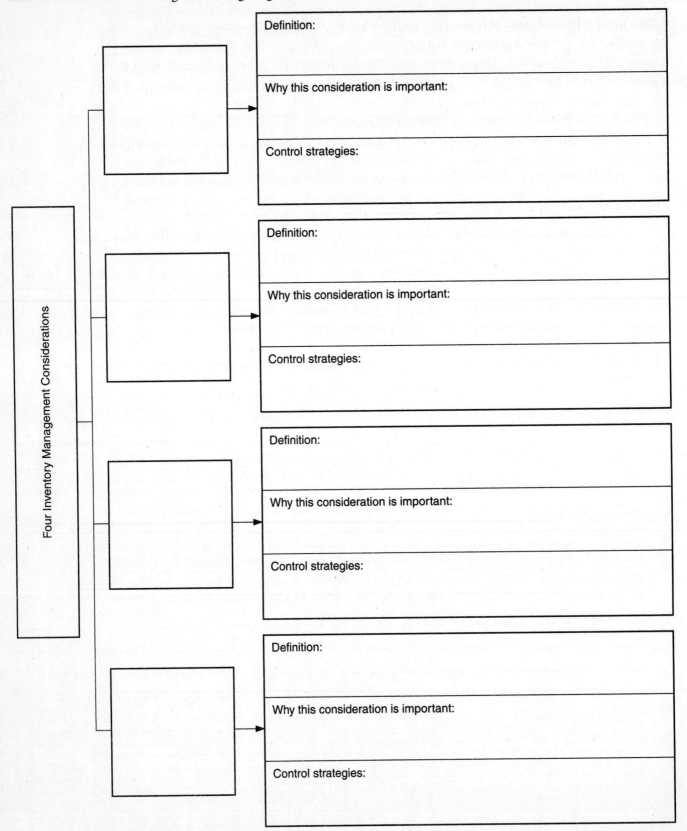

Four Inventory Management Considerations

Definition:

Why this consideration is important:

Control strategies:

Definition:

Why this consideration is important:

Control strategies:

Definition:

Why this consideration is important:

Control strategies:

Definition:

Why this consideration is important:

Control strategies:

L. Extending Knowledge: Inventory Management

Bar coding is a product identification technology that makes inventory management more efficient. It allows data to be encoded into a series of parallel bars and spaces. These codes are found on every package and on many products (including this book). When a scanning device is moved across the symbol, the pattern is analyzed by the bar code reader and translated into meaningful information. This enables the users of this technology to collect, record, and retrieve information rapidly and accurately. As a consumer, you are probably most aware of this technology as a cashier scans the price of a product into the cash register.

1. Access the Internet to answer the following questions:

   a) What year was bar coding first used commercially? (One Web site you might find this

   information is at www.adams1.com/pub/russadam/history.html.) _____

   b) How does bar coding work? _____

   _____

   _____

   _____

   c) Use Barpoint (www.barpoint.com) to decode the bar code on a purse, backpack, or any other item for which you can locate a bar code.

2. How can a retailer use bar coding technology to control the following inventory management concerns?

   Overstocks: _____

   _____

   _____

   _____

   Out-of-stocks: _____

   _____

   _____

   _____

   Shrinkage: _____

   _____

   _____

   _____

   Turnover: _____

   _____

   _____

   _____

Read Section 8.6, **Distributing to International Markets** (pages 325–327), in your textbook and fill in the missing information in the following chart.

Options for Distributing to a Foreign Market	Explanation

A freight forwarder may be hired because _____

_____

The freight forwarder's role is to:

1. _____

2. _____

3. _____

4. _____

5. _____

CIF charges are_____

N. Researching on the Internet: Distributing to International Markets

Imagine that you are a new company that needs to distribute product to an international market. Go to the Vancouver Port Authority's Web site at www.portvancouver.com to research what services are available to assist you.

1. What key benefits does the Port of Vancouver offer container customers?

_____

_____

_____

_____

_____

2. In addition to container operations, what other port services does the Port of Vancouver provide?

_____

_____

_____

_____

_____

3. What are some of the companies and agencies that could provide you with help if your company had to ship a container of goods to the Pacific Rim? Investigate two or three of these companies to find out what services they offer.

_____

_____

_____

_____

_____

4. What considerations for international shipping have you learned about on the Port of Vancouver Web site that you were not aware of before?

_____

_____

_____

_____

_____

Red Cross to the Rescue: Logistics and Distribution

The Canadian Red Cross is part of the International Red Cross Movement, which comprises 176 National Red Cross and Red Crescent Societies. The Movement is the largest disaster preparedness and relief network in the world. But what does disaster preparedness and relief really mean? What does the Canadian Red Cross do during a disaster?

The disaster recovery process begins with the "relief phase." At this stage, the Red Cross works with municipalities, governments, and other relief organizations to address immediate basic needs including shelter, clothing, food, water, first aid, and emotional support. During the next phase, the "recovery phase," the Red Cross helps people rebuild their lives and their communities by coordinating the recovery effort with other relief organizations. This ensures that any gaps in the assistance provided by municipalities, governments, and insurance companies are filled.

In recent disasters, the Red Cross has helped provide assistance in the purchase of essential household items, as well as the clothing and equipment necessary for people to return to school or work. They have helped individuals and families pay for what they need most—from groceries, clothing, and rent to emergency home repairs, transportation, household items, medicine, and tools. Depending on the situation and local agreements, the Red Cross may also open shelters for people who have been evacuated or displaced by a disaster, and provide meals and snacks to families and to emergency workers in affected areas. When necessary, the Red Cross may even help those needing long-term recovery assistance when other resources are not available or are inadequate.

But what is often overlooked is the massive effort and intensive planning that occurs behind the scenes. It would be impossible to mount an effective recovery effort if all of the planning and processes were not in place far before a disaster occurs. One of the greatest challenges is getting the resources in place quickly. In disaster situations, lives depend on rapid response. The distribution system must operate flawlessly since any delay can be extremely costly. An intense coordination effort is needed to assure the delivery of quality and timely services to those affected.

In major disasters, a disaster response team of Red Cross workers is sent to the scene. They determine the needs of the people affected and make sure that people are given shelter and feed. Many staff and volunteers provide support to the Red Cross relief operation and ensure things run smoothly—they manage warehouses where supplies are stored, procure resources, do the accounting, handle logistics, facilitate communications, and many other activities. As a result of this effort, the necessary rapid and efficient response is made possible. Other Red Cross workers serve as a link between the Red Cross relief operation and the affected community, other voluntary agencies, government, businesses, community groups, and the media. This ensures that efforts are coordinated, resources are shared, and ultimately the community is served efficiently and effectively.

1. Logistics is sometimes described as getting the right goods at the right price to the right place at the right time. Relate this to the challenges faced by the Red Cross in a disaster situation. How might a disaster place stress on supply management?

_____

_____

_____

_____

_____

_____

_____

_____

_____

_____

2. When a disaster strikes, the Canadian Red Cross solicits financial donations. Why doesn't it encourage the public to donate food, clothing, and other relief supplies?

_____

_____

_____

_____

_____

_____

_____

_____

_____

_____

3. Use the Internet to research the distribution challenges faced by relief agencies in mounting an international relief effort.

_____

_____

_____

_____

_____

_____

_____

_____

_____

_____

Word Search

Find the words listed below in the following puzzle.

```
V  K  S  I  N  E  X  L  Z  C  E  O  E  D  T  K  E  X  T  L
E  C  E  V  N  M  C  A  A  X  A  G  E  E  Z  M  I  N  Z  E
N  O  L  I  C  T  A  R  C  I  A  P  L  C  I  E  E  D  F  N
D  T  E  P  N  Q  E  L  E  K  C  E  T  T  E  M  X  M  P  N
I  S  C  S  I  T  U  R  N  M  M  R  N  A  E  K  M  M  D  A
N  F  T  B  K  S  E  I  M  A  M  I  E  G  I  F  S  V  R  H
G  O  I  Y  I  C  R  N  R  E  T  O  A  M  G  N  W  B  W  C
M  T  V  V  E  H  X  K  S  S  D  N  C  Z  O  K  V  H  E  N
A  U  E  B  S  P  E  H  U  I  A  I  A  E  O  F  I  J  U  O
C  O  E  D  T  T  H  J  J  M  V  C  A  I  A  W  N  R  G  I
H  O  U  L  I  S  P  R  Y  C  D  E  I  R  P  H  R  I  O  T
I  O  Q  N  J  L  Q  R  L  O  G  I  S  T  I  C  S  F  L  U
N  A  G  F  G  D  O  T  U  R  N  O  V  E  R  E  M  P  A  B
E  F  F  J  R  T  S  R  E  L  I  A  T  E  R  A  S  U  T  I
E  Z  C  W  N  S  R  E  L  A  S  E  L  O  H  W  B  H  A  R
V  S  P  E  C  I  A  L  T  Y  C  H  A  N  N  E  L  C  C  T
L  D  V  I  N  L  K  X  Y  C  B  K  G  A  H  E  D  H  T  S
U  N  D  S  I  R  U  B  U  J  A  S  W  I  Z  R  R  Z  W  I
I  Q  H  B  F  H  M  Y  G  F  X  P  T  K  I  N  X  U  G  D
X  K  H  T  K  D  T  O  P  T  P  K  G  N  C  M  M  U  T  K
```

captain	logistics
catalogue	out of stock
distribution channel	retailers
e-commerce	selective
exclusive	shrinkage
infomercial	specialty channel
intensive	telemarketing
intermediaries	turnover
inventory management	vending machine
just-in-time	wholesalers

Multiple Choice

Circle the best response.

1. An intermediary that buys products from domestic sources and resells them to retail stores or other businesses and industries is

    a) a broker

    b) an industrial distributor

    c) a wholesaler

    d) a rack jobber

2. A distribution policy whereby a producer sells its products or services in only one retail outlet in a particular area is

    a) an intensive distribution

    b) a selective distribution

    c) an integrated distribution

    d) an exclusive distribution

3. A distribution policy where a producer sells products in a few retail outlets in a particular area is

    a) an intensive distribution

    b) a selective distribution

    c) an integrated distribution

    d) an exclusive distribution

4. A company that can control a distribution channel is

    a) a channel captain

    b) an industrial distribution

    c) a manufacturer's agent

    d) a vertical marketing systems

5. The final link in the indirect distribution chain is the

    a) wholesaler

    b) shipper and receiver

    c) retailer

    d) consumer

True/False

Circle T if the statement is true, F if it is false.

1. Integrated distribution is an arrangement in which a business reaches buyers by employing two or more different types of channels for the same basic product.   T   F

2. Wholesalers often provide market information to retailers.   T   F

3. Manufacturers, importers, and wholesalers use catalogues to sell directly to both industrial and non-industrial consumers.   T   F

Fill in the Blanks

1. _____ describes a situation where the manufacturer, distributor, or retailer owns both distribution outlets and manufacturing facilities for a product or a line of products.

2. A marketing channel where producers and ultimate consumers interact directly with each other is a _____ channel.

3. Marketers who use the Internet to sell their products are engaging in _____.

4. A marketing channel where intermediaries are situated between producers and consumers is a _____ distribution channel.

5. _____ is the process of designing and managing a supply chain.

Q. Marketing Plan: Distribution

For your product, service, idea, or cause develop a distribution strategy. (Remember, you may use more than one type of distribution channel.)

Considerations	Response for Your Product, Service, Idea, or Cause
Is the channel directed at an industrial and/or institutional consumer?	
What is the income level of the target market?	
How large is the local market?	
What are the buying habits of the consumers?	
Will the selected channel reach a sufficient number of consumers?	
Is it a seasonal or high fashion item?	
Can the channel become a competitive advantage?	
Is the product custom made?	
Will the product spoil?	
What is the unit value of the product?	
How large or heavy is the product?	
Does the product come with a manufacturer's warranty?	
Is the product price sensitive?	

Channels of Distribution

Explain whether you would adopt a policy of intensive, selective, exclusive, or integrated distribution.

_____

_____

_____

_____

_____

_____

Types of Channels

Explain the type of distribution channel that you would use: direct, indirect (specify), specialized (specify), or a combination. _____

_____

_____

_____

_____

_____

_____

Logistics and Inventory Management

List and explain any logistical and inventory management considerations that you might need to consider.

_____

_____

_____

_____

_____

_____

_____

Distributing to International Markets

Will you be distributing internationally? If so, what distribution option(s) might you consider? Why?

_____

_____

_____

_____

_____

_____

_____

CHAPTER 9: Advertising, Promotion, and Sales

A. Understanding Key Terms: Chapter Introduction

Before reading this chapter, write what you think each term means in the middle column of this chart. After reading this chapter, complete the column on the right. How do your definitions and the textbook's compare?

Term	What Do You Think It Means?	Definition from Text
brand awareness		
endorsement		
copywriter		
SWOT analysis		
emotional appeals		
rational appeals		
direct-to-home advertising		
targeted campaigns		
publicity		
press releases		
rebate		

B. Understanding the Ideas: 9.1 The Importance of Advertising

As you read Section 9.1, **The Importance of Advertising** (pages 335–343), in your textbook, complete the following.

Advertising is important because _it shows the general public the benifits of a certain product and shows why the certain product is better than the competition. It can advertise to a certain market and Explain its product._

Advertising is most important for products and services that are:

In a market where their is

The goals of advertising are:

Goal	Explanation

C. Explaining Examples: The Goals of Advertising

For each of the following advertisements, identify and explain what the goal is.

Advertisement	Goal
a headache pill advertisement claims it is the "number one" remedy recommended by doctors	A pill to cure a headache, tries to sell its product by stating that doctors use it.
an advertisement for a 50-year-old canned soup uses nostalgia for the "good old days"	Reminding the adults that used to eat the soup when they were children.
a detergent advertisement provides a coupon for 70¢ off the next purchase	Coupon may attract customers to buy their product
a cell phone advertisement repeatedly uses the phrase "meet our newest…"	Starting their new models that have just come out.
an amusement park is advertised as "not just for the kids, but for the young at heart"	that the amusement park can be fun for adults and not only children.
a sports star is featured in an advertisement for a sports shoe brand	To attract people by using a famous athlete to sell shoes.
an Internet advertisement for a new airline offers a fare discount for tickets purchased online	Attract people to buy tickets online and by using their advertisment.
an advertisement for a new soap claims its product is the only one that has the benefit of reversing skin aging	The soap can help people look younger.
an advertisement for a 75-year-old cookie uses "grandma's recipe" as a selling point	Children and parents may want to remember their grandmas recipe and try it.
a life insurance advertisement, previously targetted at the "over 50" now uses a young, 30-something spokesperson	To attract the adults aged under 50 years of age to purchase life insurance.

Read Section 9.2, **Creating the Message** (pages 345–352), in your textbook and complete the following.

Intent

Good advertising has a goal or a _____ _____. The company that owns the product,

service, or idea to be advertised generally determines the _____ of an _____.

The company often gives the job of _____, _____, and _____

the effectiveness of an advertisement to an _____ _____ .

Advertising agency teams consist of three main players: _____ _____,

_____, and _____ _____.

Message

Translating the client's intent into an effective message requires three major steps:

1. _____

2. _____

3. _____

USP is _____

_____

SWOT analysis stands for _____

Selecting the Appeal

Appeal	Focus of Appeal

E. Analyzing Advertisements: Selecting the Appeal

Collect and analyze one ad for each of the four appeals (biological, emotional, rational, and social). Collect one additional ad that appeals specifically to you and explain which of the four appeals it is using. Fill in the chart below to complete your analysis.

Advertisement	Target Market	Advertising Goal	Advertising Appeal	Overall Effectiveness

Advertising, Promotion, and Sales

Read Section 9.3, **Selecting the Media** (pages 353–356), in your textbook and use the following to help guide your notetaking.

A _____ carries a message to an audience.

Factors Used to Determine Medium

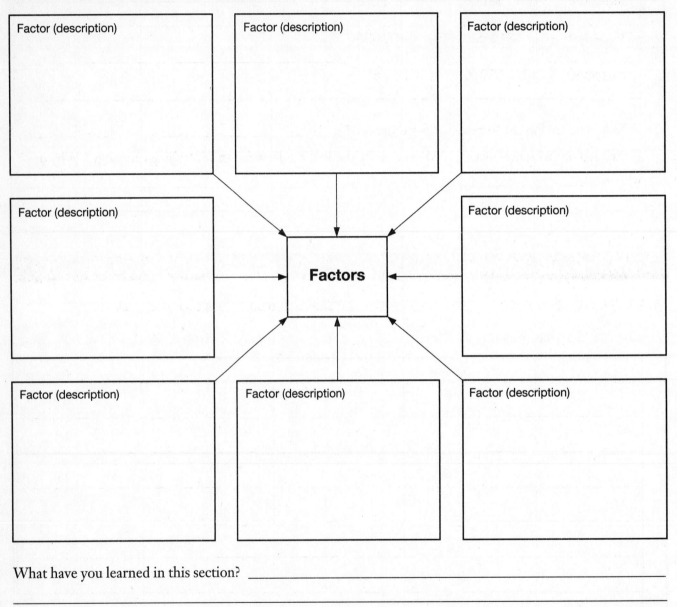

Factor (description)

Factor (description)

Factor (description)

Factor (description)

Factors

Factor (description)

Factor (description)

Factor (description)

Factor (description)

What have you learned in this section? _____

_____

_____

_____

_____

_____

_____

G. Calculating Costs

1. Calculate the following. Use the space provided to show your work.

Medium	Cost	Audience	CPM
FM radio	$500	2000	
magazine	$3000	9000	
TV show	$10 000	30 000	
newspaper	$5000	12 500	

2. Which medium has the lowest cost per thousand? _____

3. Is the medium with the lowest CPM necessarily the best medium for an advertising campaign? Why or why not? _____

_____

H. Making Assessments: Factors Used to Determine Medium

As a small flower shop owner, you have a limited budget and staff to promote a two-week sale.

1. Consider each of the factors to determine which advertising medium you would use.

Factor	Assessment

2. Based on your assessment of each factor, what would you select as your medium? Why? _____

_____

_____

Read the article and then answer the questions that follow.

Cinema Advertising Comes of Age

By Nate Hendley

Cinema advertising is on a roll. In fact, cinema ads have "probably had a greater accelerated growth in the last few years than any other medium in the country," says Brian Stewart, CEO of Tribute Entertainment Media Group in Toronto.

According to Stewart, spending on cinema advertising—a broad genre that covers everything from films and slides to posters, theatre promotions, ads printed on movie tickets, and so on—has grown to $25 million to $30 million a year in Canada. That's up spectacularly from just $1 million or $2 million in the mid-1980s when the medium really got going. He predicts that the market for cinema ads will continue to expand, perhaps doubling in size within a few years.

Of that total spending of $25 million to $30 million, full-motion on-screen ads account for $15 million to $16 million, estimates Stewart…. He says slides on screen, motionless images projected on the screen, come in at "a very distant second."…

Although full-motion on-screen ads dominate the medium, slides do have some advantages. For one thing, they're cheap: A four-week campaign featuring a 60-second full-motion on-screen ad, shown on 1172 screens at 196 Cineplex Odeon theatres, will cost advertisers $296 500 if they pay according to the rate card. A four-week slides on screen campaign, shown on 671 screens at 95 Cineplex Odeon theatres, costs only about a 10th of that: just $30 000.

For small businesses, "slides are the way to go, because the production and distribution costs are so low," says Ken Prue, director of marketing and communications at Galaxy Entertainment in Toronto….

The obvious drawback to slides on screen is that they offer "a static image," says Stewart. "They don't move, don't have sound," both of which minimize their appeal.

Full-motion ads suffer from no such limitations; most are 60 to 90 seconds long, versus the most common 30-second format for a TV spot, and provide kinetic visuals with an audio accompaniment. Throw in a captive audience and engaging content, and you've got a very powerful advertising medium.

To be effective, full-motion ads have to be energetic, entertaining, and focused on "phantasmagoric things that really punch on a 50-foot screen with Dolby Digital or THX or Surround Sound," says Prue….

Surveys suggest that full-motion cinema ads generate higher recall than TV and radio. One done in 2000 for Cineplex Odeon by Thompson Lightstone and Co. of Toronto looked at "total recall" (the ability to remember an ad, with or without memory clues) among 323 patrons of film, TV, and radio in Toronto, Vancouver, and Calgary. Full-motion movie ads enjoyed a 74% average recall rate (the combined total for aided plus unaided recall). This was compared with figures of 37% for radio and 32% for television, according to research by the ComQUEST division of BBM Bureau of Measurement in Toronto….

[T]he market for cinema ads remains small compared to that of other media….

One reason is a limitation of the medium. "As a stand-alone medium, you're not going to get massive reach, like you would with outdoor or newspaper," states Bruce Claassen, president of Genesis Media in Toronto. "This is because there's only so much of the population that goes to movies in any given week."

Cineplex Odeon estimates that 3.6 million moviegoers will view one of their 60-second full-motion spots during a month-long campaign. An impressive figure, until you consider that popular TV shows can attract the same number of Canadian viewers in one evening.

Unlike television, radio, or the Internet, however, full-motion ads enjoy the benefit of a built-in audience that's guaranteed to pay attention whenever they're broadcast.

There's no "zipping and zapping" in a theatre, says Paul Bolte (director of national sales cinema marketing for Cineplex Odeon in Toronto). Once the lights go down, patrons have little choice but to watch whatever comes on screen. That's an important consideration for advertisers facing an increasingly fractured media universe.

In a movie theatre, "none of the 400 people have a converter in their hands, and the fridge is a mile away," says Prue. "They are watching and listening."

Source: Excerpts from Marketing Magazine, *May 6, 2002.*

1. How much is spent on cinema advertising? How much of an increase is that from the 1980s? _____
   _____
   _____
   _____
   _____
   _____

2. What are some examples of cinema advertising that is used? _____
   _____
   _____
   _____
   _____
   _____
   _____

3. What are the advantages of slides? _____
   _____
   _____
   _____
   _____
   _____
   _____
   _____

4. What are the advantages of cinema ads? _____
   _____
   _____
   _____
   _____
   _____

5. What are the disadvantages of cinema ads? _____
   _____
   _____
   _____
   _____
   _____

Read Section 9.4, **Types of Media** (pages 357–367), in your textbook, and use the following chart to make notes on the advantages and disadvantages of each of the main advertising media.

Medium (description)	Advantages	Disadvantages

K. Applying Knowledge: Types of Media

Which type of medium might be most suitable for promoting each of the following? Provide a brief rationale for each. (Hint: There may be more than one medium for each.)

Product/Service	Rationale
0% financing on an automobile	
greeting cards	
a weekend sale at an outlet mall	
a local grocery store	
a dog-walking service	
clothing targeted at the teen market	
a new skin moisturizing lotion targeted at women aged 20–45	

Advertising, Promotion, and Sales

Read the article and then answer the questions that follow.

Why Print Promotes Itself Through TV

By Chris Powell

Nearly 30 years after his historic goal in the 1972 Summit Series, Canadian hockey legend Paul Henderson looks grey, wrinkled…and several tonnes over his playing weight.

"The Goal" is once again receiving significant airplay, sort of, in a TV commercial for the Canadian Magazine Publishers Association. Created by Toronto's One Company, the spot hilariously marries hall-of-fame broadcaster Foster Hewitt's actual play-by-play of the Henderson goal to video footage of soccer-playing elephants.

The ad ends with the tag line "It's not the same if it's not Canadian" and urges viewers to "Get the genuine article. Read a Canadian magazine." That's followed by a Web site address, www.genuinearticle.ca, where viewers can find subscription and content information for up to 185 participating Canadian magazines.

Maureen Cavan, project director, national circulation and promotion program for the CMPA in Toronto, says the ad… —has led to "tens of thousands" of hits on the Web site since it began airing in March.

While TV ads for print properties aren't new, they have become increasingly prevalent after recent media mergers that saw daily newspapers like the *Globe and Mail* and *National Post* brought into corporate families that also include network and specialty TV channels….

This increased TV exposure for the *Globe* and *Post* is part of the reason behind the *Toronto Star*'s decision to launch its own $2-million TV campaign last fall….

Victor Kruklis, VP of marketing and planning for the *Star*, says he operates on the principle of "no free rein over contested turf." In a nutshell, this means that since both the *Globe* and *Post* now have easier access to broadcast advertising, the *Star* must follow suit….

But for all his talk about contested turf, Kruklis acknowledges that TV advertising is also an effective means of reaching would-be *Star* readers in Canada's most populated urban market.

"There is a portion of the population that doesn't read. We acknowledge that, and that's who we're trying to talk to," he says. "The higher the socio-economic status, the more likely they are to read newspapers, but even within good demographics, there are non-readers or infrequent readers. And we're trying to get a message to them from as many different sources as we can, to say, 'Come take another look at us.' "

TV's high production values, its ability to match poignant images with evocative music…can make it possible to make even the *Backwater Gazette* look like the *Wall Street Journal* with a sufficient budget.

But the key to successful TV advertising for print is making sure the ads don't promise more than the print property can deliver, says Rachael MacKenzie, director of marketing for the news and business group at Rogers Publishing in Toronto, which includes *Maclean's* (Rogers also owns *Marketing*). "I think if you've in any way oversold on TV, that's just bad creative," she says. "If somebody picks up *Maclean's* after they see a TV spot that we do and they're profoundly disappointed by what they see or read, then we haven't done our job right." …

According to the CMPA's Cavan, the relatively recent advent of specialty channels has made it easier for magazines to purchase TV advertising for print properties, because specialties' niche programming fits perfectly with the specialized nature of magazines….

"I would say that (specialty TV) has made choosing TV as a vehicle for promotion easier than it might have been in the past," Cavan explains. "It's the best way to reach a target of magazine readers. When they watch television they're more likely to watch specialty channels, because they're readers first and television viewers second."

But while the response to the CMPA ads is a fitting testament to the power of TV advertising, Cavan is quick to point out that the spots are just one component in the organization's new $5.5-million marketing campaign, which also includes print, direct mail, and in-store marketing.

"Television is being used not as a direct sales agent for the product, but to warm up the audience to recognize the benefits of subscribing to or purchasing Canadian magazines," says Cavan.

And for all its strengths, TV advertising has one major drawback: It's costly.

"An independent publisher can afford only a small presence on television," says Cavan, who says the CMPA campaign is possible only because of the participation of several magazine publishers. "The opportunity to have a large-scale TV campaign is restricted to very few."

Source: Excerpts from Marketing Magazine, *May 6, 2002.*

1. Why has there been a sudden surge of television advertisements among newspapers and magazines?

   _____

   _____

   _____

   _____

   _____

   _____

   _____

   _____

   _____

2. List the strengths and weaknesses of television advertisements as discussed in the article.

   _____

   _____

   _____

   _____

   _____

   _____

   _____

   _____

   _____

   _____

   _____

   _____

   _____

   _____

   _____

   _____

   _____

   _____

M. Understanding the Ideas: 9.5 Publicity and Public Relations

Read Section 9.5, **Publicity and Public Relations** (pages 368–370), in your textbook and use the following to help guide your notetaking.

Publicity is defined as _____

_____

_____

The Functions of a Public Relations Company	
Function	**Explanation**

What have you learned in this section? _____

_____

_____

_____

N. Analyzing Examples: Publicity and Public Relations

Find an example of each of the following. Briefly explain how each is a form of publicity or public relations.

Example	Explanation
a press release about a positive thing that a company is doing	
a press conference at which media representatives are allowed to ask questions	
a copy of a corporation's annual report	
a lobby group in the news	
crisis management	

O. Creating a Press Release: Media Relations

Create a press release for the media in your community. Your press release must have a headline, contact information, and release time at the top of the page. Remember that the writing style should be in the form of a news story. Give it news value. Keep it concise and precise, and make it grammatically correct. Before beginning this exercise, complete the following steps.

Identify a current or future event in the life of your school or in your community that you would like to profile.

_____

Identify your audience for the press release. _____

Choose the information that your audience needs to make a decision to support the ideas contained within the press release. _____

_____

_____

Advertising, Promotion, and Sales

Read Section 9.6, **Sales Promotion** (pages 370–376), in your textbook and complete the following.

Sales promotion consists of _____

_____

_____

_____

Businesses use sales promotion to:

_____

_____

_____

_____

_____

_____

_____

_____

_____

Methods of Promotion

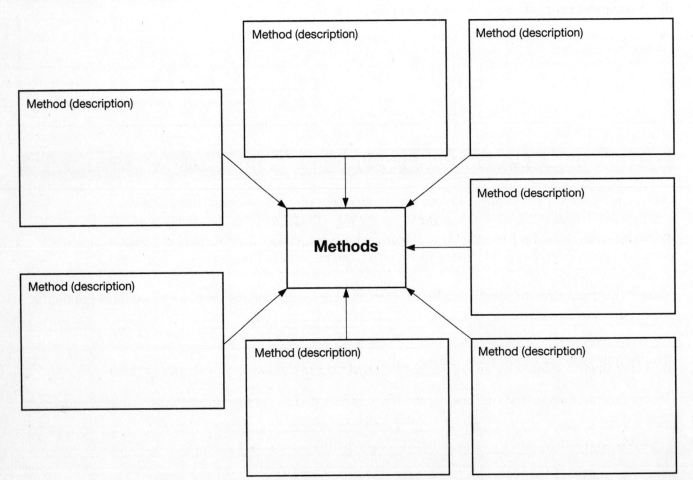

For each of the following, identify and explain the sales promotion activity.

a)   A software package contains a form for the buyer to fill out and send to the software company to receive $15:

_____

_____

_____

_____

b)   A rental car company's Web site provides a document that could be printed and presented to the company
      for a discount on vehicle rental: _____

_____

_____

_____

c)   A coffee shop is attracting customers with its "Alaskan Cruise for Two" prize: _____

_____

_____

_____

d)   A computer store offers customers a free mouse upon purchases of $50 or more: _____

_____

_____

_____

e)   A men's wear store flyer reads "All summer stock must go—up to 50% discount on all items": _____

_____

_____

_____

_____

f)   A pharmacy has a special rack with a two-in-one toothpaste/mouthwash product set at its checkouts: ____

_____

_____

_____

_____

g)   Newspaper employees are giving out free copies of the paper at bus stops and grocery stores: _____

_____

_____

_____

_____

As you read Section 9.7, **Personal Selling** (pages 376–382), in your textbook, fill in the following and complete the chart.

A sale is _____

Personal selling occurs when _____

The amount of personal selling that is required depends on _____

_____

_____

_____

_____

Steps in the Sales Process

Description

↓

Description

↓

Description

↓

Description

↓

Description

↓

Description

↓

Description

You are a sales associate for a brand of digital camera, DVD, or another electronic product of your choosing. Gather as much information as possible about the brand (e.g., features, benefits, price, etc.). Then complete the following chart to begin selling the product to a customer.

Your product: _____

Step in the Sales Process	How to Apply This Step to Your Product

T. Reviewing the Chapter

Multiple Choice

Circle the best response.

1. Which of the following often uses celebrities to endorse a brand?

   a) brand awareness and positioning

   b) brand trial

   c) brand preference

   d) brand reminder and repositioning

2. Which of the following appeals stresses convenience, cost savings, safety, warranties, and ease of purchase?

   a) emotional appeals

   b) rational appeals

   c) biological appeals

   d) social appeals

3. Which of the following factors determine whether or not a specific medium is appropriate for a specific message or a specific audience?

   a) reach, frequency, selectivity, durability, lead-time, mechanical requirements, clutter, and costs

   b) reach, frequency, selectivity, profit, lead-time, mechanical requirements, clutter, and costs

   c) reach, frequency, selectivity, durability, lead-time, mechanical requirements, clutter, and projected sales

   d) none of the above

4. Aggregate campaigns use

   a) magazine subscription lists, newspaper birth notices, credit reports

   b) local distribution companies or telemarketers

   c) both a) and b)

   d) none of the above

5. A public relations company coordinates all of the following functions, EXCEPT

   a) media relations

   b) lobbying

   c) crisis management

   d) personal selling

6. Refunds and rebates are an example of

   a) sales promotion

   b) public relations

   c) advertising

   d) media selection

7. Low-cost pens placed in special racks at the checkout point of a store is an example of

   a) samples

   b) special sales

   c) point-of-purchase display

   d) premiums and self-liquidators

8. The third step in the sales process is

   a) presenting the product

   b) determining the customer's wants

   c) making the approach

   d) handling objections

True/False

State whether the statement is true (T) or false (F).

_____ Most brand trial advertising uses sales promotion to directly influence consumers to purchase.

_____ Advertisements stressing the convenience, cost, and savings is an emotional appeal.

_____ Frequency is the number of people exposed to a message.

_____ External clutter occurs when an advertisement must compete with other ads on the same page.

_____ Acquiring product knowledge is the first step in a successful sales process.

_____ Lower priced products require a higher degree of selling.

Matching

Draw a line from the concept on the left to the advertising appeal on the right.

"Tired of the acne on your face? Use Product Y."　　　　biological appeal

"Of all the cars tested, Auto G is the safest."　　　　emotional appeal

"Use Brand X to live longer and stay healthier."　　　　rational appeal

"Use Candy Z to remember the times when you were a child."　　　　social appeal

U. Marketing Plan: Advertising, Promotion, and Sales

Read page 386 in your textbook, **Marketing Plan**. Use the following to determine advertising, publicity, and promotional opportunities for your product, service, idea, or cause.

What is the product?	
Who is the target market?	
What are its benefits to the target market?	
What media and advertising venues would be appropriate?	
What are the reach and frequency for each medium?	
What is the cost of each ad or promotion for each medium?	
What goals will be accomplished by using this strategy?	

Do a **SWOT** analysis on your promotion strategy.

a) Strengths:_____

   _____

   _____

b) Weaknesses: _____

   _____

   _____

c) Opportunities:_____

   _____

   _____

d) Threats: _____

   _____

   _____

Credits

Chapter 1 What Is Marketing?

p. 4   Hi & Lois cartoon by Mort Walker & Dik Browne. Reprinted with special permission of King Features Syndicate.

p. 13   Article: "From Recalled to Requested" by Stephen Abbott, *Marketing Magazine*, March 11, 2002, p.18. Reprinted by permission of *Marketing Magazine*.

Chapter 2 The Consumer

p. 26   Article: "Forget the hip, focus on the oldsters with money" by Mark Solomons and Annie Counsell, *Financial Post*, February 5, 2001, E8. Source: *Financial Times* (London). © 2001 Financial Times (London).

Chapter 3 The Competitive Market

p. 52   Table. Source: Adapted from "The Canadian Soft Drink Market: Sales Volume & Per Capita Consumption by Region", based on data from the Statistics Canada publications "Food Consumption in Canada: Part I", Catalogue 32–229, "Food Consumption in Canada: Part II", Catalogue 32–230, and Post Censal Estimates, 2000. *Statistics Canada information is used with the permission of the Minister of Industry, as Minister responsible for Statistics Canada. Information on the availability of the wide range of data from Statistics Canada can be obtained from Statistics Canada's Regional Offices, its World Wide Web site at http://www.statcan.ca, and its toll-free access number 1-800-263-1136.*

p. 53   Graph. Source: "Top 30 Countries—Soft Drink Consumption" published at the Canadian Soft Drink Association Web site (www.softdrink.ca/tp100sde.htm). Copyright © 1996–2002 Canadian Soft Drink Association (CSDA). All rights reserved.

pp. 54–55   Article: "Falling profits tarnish Golden Arches" by Jennifer Wells, *The Toronto Star*, May 30, 2002, pp. D1, D13. Reprinted with permission—The Toronto Star Syndicate.

Chapter 4 Marketing Research

p. 67   Article: Census as Secondary Market Research. Source: "Selling the census" by Catherine Porter, *The Toronto Star*, July 14, 2002, pp. C1, C5. Reprinted by permission—The Toronto Star Syndicate.

p. 76   Table. Source: Adapted from "Advertising Agency Salaries ($000s)—Agency Size," *Marketing Magazine*, October 29, 2001. Reprinted by permission of *Marketing Magazine*.

Chapter 5 Product Development

p. 90   Article: "Footless, bulge-free and rich to boot: Turning a simple idea into a million-dollar business" by Jennifer Wells, *The Toronto Star*, May 25, 2002, pp. D1, D5. Reprinted by permission—The Toronto Star Syndicate.

p. 92   Cartoon: *Helen, Sweetheart of the Internet*, June 22, 2002. Copyright © Tribune Media Service, Inc. All Rights Reserved. Reprinted with Permission.

Chapter 6 Positioning and Branding

p. 111   Greyhound Lines, Inc. logo. Copyright © 2002 Greyhound Lines, Inc. All rights reserved. Reprinted by permission of Greyhound Lines, Inc.; World Wildlife Fund Canada logo. © 1986 Panda symbol WWF ® WWF Registered Trademark; Apple logo. Apple and the Apple logo are trademarks of Apple Computer, Inc., registered in the U.S. and other countries, used with permission.

p. 117   Article: "Pampers took rebranding to heart" by Danny Kucharsky, *Marketing Magazine*, June 25, 2001. Reprinted by permission of *Marketing Magazine*.

Chapter 7 Pricing

p. 131   Report: "Vitamin price-fixing" by Erica Johnson, CBC Marketplace, Air Date: April 10, 2001. Copyright CBC/SRC, 2002. All Rights Reserved.

Chapter 9 Advertising, Promotion, and Sales

p. 174   Article: "Cinema Advertising Comes of Age" by Nate Hendley, *Marketing Magazine*, May 6, 2002, p. 16. Reprinted by permission of *Marketing Magazine*.

p. 178   Article: "Why Print Promotes Itself Through TV" by Chris Powell, *Marketing Magazine*, May 6, 2002, p. 20. Reprinted by permission of *Marketing Magazine*.

MANAWIS SECONDARY
12800 - 68 Avenue
Surrey, B.C. V3W 2A8

S SECONDARY
- 66 Avenue
, B.C. V3W 2A8

S SECONDARY
- 66 Avenue
, B.C. V3W 2A8